As Good As Any

Contributions to the Study of
Mass Media and Communications

News of Crime: Courts and Press in Conflict
J. Edward Gerald

As Good As Any

FOREIGN CORRESPONDENCE ON AMERICAN RADIO, 1930–1940

DAVID H. HOSLEY

CONTRIBUTIONS TO THE STUDY OF
MASS MEDIA AND COMMUNICATIONS, NUMBER 2

Greenwood Press
WESTPORT, CONNECTICUT · LONDON, ENGLAND

Library of Congress Cataloging in Publication Data

Hosley, David H.
  As good as any.

  (Contributions to the study of mass media and
communications, ISSN 0732-4456; no. 2)
  Bibliography: p.
  Includes index.
  1. Radio journalism—United States—History.
  2. Foreign news—United States—History. 3. Foreign
correspondents—United States—Biography. I. Title.
  II. Series.
  PN4888.R33H67 1984   070.1'9   83-12730
  ISBN 0-313-23782-4 (lib. bdg.)

Library of Congress Catalog Card Number: 83-12730
ISBN: 0-313-23782-4
ISSN: 0732-4456

First published in 1984

Greenwood Press
A division of Congressional Information Service, Inc.
88 Post Road West
Westport, Connecticut 06881

Printed in the United States of America

10 9 8 7 6 5 4 3 2 1

Copyright Acknowledgments

   The author and publisher are grateful for permission to reprint from the
following works.
   Eric Sevareid, *Not So Wild a Dream* (New York: Knopf, 1941). Reprinted by
permission of the author.
   William L. Shirer, *Berlin Diary* (New York: Knopf, 1941). Reprinted by
permission of the author.
   Every reasonable effort has been made to trace the owners of copyright
materials in this book, but in some instances this has proven impossible. The
publishers will be glad to receive information leading to more complete
acknowledgments in subsequent printings of the book and in the meantime
extend their apologies for any omissions.

FOR MY TEACHERS

· Contents

· Preface

This book is the product of research in three cities, over five years. But its genesis goes back to some of my classes at Stanford University, where *Due to Circumstances Beyond Our Control* and *Prime Time* were required reading.

James Clerk-Maxwell, a physicist whose work with electricity led to important developments in the technical aspect of broadcasting, told his students that if they wanted to understand physics, they should learn about the history of their science.

I hope that a history of foreign correspondence, as it developed in the first dozen years of network radio in America, will help broadcast journalists better understand their profession. Too many of us have no understanding of the evolution of broadcast news. Many of the standards we live by today were established by the men and women who worked for the networks in the 1930s. This book is an attempt to identify those pioneers and to describe their techniques and values.

I owe a debt to those who helped me mold my interest in the history of broadcast news into the final product, in particular, W. Phillips Davison. Had I followed his gentle urgings more precisely, and with greater speed, this would have been a better book, and certainly a more quickly completed one.

Sigmund Diamond taught me many of the historical methods used in my research; the tools for digging were provided by him. The mistakes are mine. David Culbert, who is an authority on broadcast history at Louisiana State University, took an active interest in my work after I sent him a letter of inquiry. He has been a tremendous source of information and encouragement.

Mark Johnson, Robert Cohen, and Phyllis Endreny formed a support group, and they read many parts of my manuscript in its early form. I am grateful for their ideas and moral support.

My wife, Gayle Yamada, assisted me in the laborious task of typing these several drafts, often after putting in a twelve-hour day as an assignment editor or news director. More than that, she provided the encouragement so important in the day-to-day writing. She understood when I dwelled on the cracks in the ceiling instead of my typing, and she also understood when the repair of those cracks, and other chores, were put off.

My parents, Tom and Virginia Hosley, provided the basis for my journalistic inquiry in the first place—a home in which a love of knowledge and understanding was ever present. They have continued to support those values long after I have stopped residing there.

Finally, thanks to some journalism mentors. Arthur C. Youngberg read my first handwritten copy for the *Paso Robles Daily Press*, and corrected it with a red pen. For all of my teenage years, he was my editor; he allowed me to earn the experience which gave me a headstart and which continues to pay dividends. Jules Dundes was willing to share the knowledge he earned as a CBS executive with the students at Stanford University. His feeling about the excellence sought by the broadcasters where he worked in the 1930s pointed me toward this period as a research topic.

Norm Woodruff was the news director at KCBS when I started work there. His active interest in a group of young editors at Newsradio 74 has had a lasting impression on all of us, and I try to share with my young newspeople the keen desire he had to master the ways of covering a story as well as how to run a newsroom.

David McElhatton taught me a good detail about writing. He taught me more about putting people in your stories, and demanding the best of yourself and others. Bonnie Chastain helped educate me about the woman's place in broadcast journalism, and I admire her most for not accepting other people's ideas of what that place should be. To all of these people I owe more thanks than I can express.

Thanks also to Ralph Lowenstein and Paul Smeyak at the College of Journalism and Communications of the University of Florida for their encouragement of my interest in research.

· Introduction

The foreign correspondence heard on American network radio in the summer of 1940 has been described as a Camelot—a time when the men, the instrument, and the moment were perfectly met. Today we tend to remember the men, and give less thought to the instrument and the moment when recalling that period of broadcast foreign correspondence.

Television has assumed primacy in American broadcasting, and radio is of secondary status now. World War II for many is only glimpsed in film clips, the subject of war stories of a passing generation, the time teachers somehow never get to in modern history courses. New world crises have replaced Vienna and Munich twenty times over.

What has endured, however, are the names and faces of the men who made their mark on broadcast foreign correspondence in the years before the United States entered the war. Ed Murrow is the best remembered, the most well known newscaster in America at the time of his death in 1965. Eric Sevareid was part of the evening news on television until 1977. Howard K. Smith was nearly as visible, and Charles Collingwood, Winston Burdett, Robert Trout, and other members of "Murrow's Boys" had long careers on radio and television. William Shirer did not broadcast long after the war, but his books kept him in the public's mind.

So it was their work after the war, then, just as much as during or before the war, which gave them an enduring luster. Only John MacVane, of the NBC staff prior to 1941, had a lengthy career in broadcasting after the war.

There were others, women included, who made significant contributions to the development of foreign correspondence on radio. For the most part, the broadcasts of 1939 and 1940 were not only the highlights of their careers, they were the major part of their broadcast careers. But Tom Grandin, Fred Bate, and Max Jordan do belong next to Sevareid, Shirer, and Murrow when considering the development of foreign correspondence on the American networks. Mary Marvin Breckinridge, Betty Wason, Cecil Brown, Paul Archinard, and Helen Hiett are among those who should also be credited with significant contributions.

If generalities can be made, then some things can be said about the people who pioneered this effort. They were almost all Americans who had grown up distant from the East Coast. For the most part, they were young, in their twenties, and strong. Often newly married, they left the United States for Europe with their best years ahead of them. A remarkable number of them were Rhodes Scholars. All of them were college educated, but had not studied at Harvard or Yale, but at Washington State, Coe College, or the University of Minnesota.

If one person stood out from the group, it was Murrow. He was one of the few who went to Europe with a job in hand; the others took advantage of being in the right place at the right time. Murrow did too, but he went to London expecting to do that. Murrow was also one of the few who was not trained in journalism. His background was in public speaking and drama. That lack of formal training galled some of his colleagues, but being without preconceptions may have allowed him greater innovation.

There is some feeling that Murrow was the difference between the coverage CBS provided from overseas, and NBC's coverage. Mutual was only a minor factor. The point of this book is not to judge that one was better, but to offer as much information as possible about foreign correspondence on radio in the years 1930 through 1940.

Some of the broadcasters, and their networks, did better jobs of documenting their work than others. In doing research of the kind involved in this work, there are bound to be some errors, and more often, arguable points of emphasis. But there should also be a wealth of information not previously reported, and certainly not gathered in one book. It is hoped that this effort will serve those who read it well.

As Good As Any

1 · Precursors

For months, Cecil Brown had been trying to convince Columbia Broadcasting System officials that he should be hired as the CBS Rome correspondent. It was 1939, and the continued growth of the Nazi Axis and the death of the Pope underlined the need for a network correspondent in Italy. CBS had just added Eric Sevareid to work with Thomas Grandin in Paris. Edward R. Murrow had been the CBS European director since early 1937, and William L. Shirer had joined the network in September of that year to handle broadcasts from the continent.

The Austrian and Munich crises of 1938 established the need for full-time correspondents, but even toward the end of 1939, Murrow and his assistants found themselves, like NBC's duo of Fred Bate and Max Jordan, setting up concerts and cultural talks to be broadcast back to America.

Brown had worked part-time for CBS to arrange broadcasts from Rome. The Sistine Chapel Choir was popular. He also arranged for newspapermen, such as Herbert Matthews, to broadcast reports for CBS. But the print organization bosses were not enthusiastic about hearing their reporters reveal information over the airwaves hours before readers could see it in the papers, and most of the newspaper and wire service staffers had been forbidden to broadcast.

Brown called Murrow and tried to convince him that the only way CBS was going to receive reports from Rome was by having its own man, and Brown wanted the job. Brown was an International News Service reporter and had no experience in broadcasting. But neither Shirer nor Sevareid had any, and they were working out well for the network. Murrow took Brown aboard and arranged his first broadcast, which was done in January 1940.

The broadcast, like the rest of those from Europe to the United States, was arranged through the government broadcasting agency. As Brown put on earphones to take his cue, he could hear Shirer in Berlin complete his report and throw the network back to New York. The network announcer then introduced Brown, giving his name the British pronunciation. Brown was an American, and had been called Cecil, as in *diesel*, all his life. But he was so nervous about his debut that he took the cue and identified himself as Cecil, as in *vessel*, Brown, and went on with his broadcast. To this day, he goes by the pronunciation given him that day in 1940 by a network announcer who figured he was introducing an Englishman.

The transformation in broadcast foreign correspondence heard in America in those years was not as sudden, but it was equally enduring. By the end of 1940, NBC and CBS—and to a lesser extent, Mutual—had established the broadcast foreign correspondent as a staple of the American news scene. The small group of men and women were as good as any radio or television foreign correspondents since, and they were a key element in the Golden Age of Radio.

In many ways, there were no role models for the radio foreign correspondents. But the foreign reporters for newspapers during the previous century had left their marks on journalism, and Joseph Matthews noted a difference between American correspondents and ones from other countries. "In war as in peace the press of a country reflects the characteristics of the society in which it is a part. In sharp contrast to the dignified professionalism of the Europeans, the Americans reported wars as they fought them: they ignored rules and precedents, introduced a spirit of competition unknown to the European press, and welcomed rough writers as enthusiastically as rough riders."[1]

To this extent, what Matthews said about the print foreign correspondents is true about those in radio: they reflected American values, they were innovators in the broadcast coverage of foreign news, and they vied with each other for exclusivity, although they often cooperated in order to get stories on the air.

The idea that the radio foreign correspondents should be

Americans was not fully developed until after World War II began. But the reasoning of NBC News Director Abe Schechter is put forth in his novel *Go Ahead Garrison!: A Story of News Broadcasting*: "The local boys can't seem to get the ABC idea through their heads. They think nothing of a couple of minutes of dead air. On an ad lib show, for instance, they'll say 'Stand by, please,' and take a leisurely look at their notes to figure out what comes next. They know news, but have no sense of showmanship or drama. And when it's time for tea—well, they just walk out. I'd like to have one of our own bunch around, Garrison."[2]

That brief example of dialogue between a network news director and one of his reporters reveals a multitude of prejudices apparently held by Schechter. It also reflects the very real differences between American and British attitudes toward broadcast news. The British had more allies in that regard than the Americans.

By 1940, Germany was using shortwave transmitters to send hours of propaganda each day toward Britain, the United States, and other targeted countries. So was Italy. Britain was not offering a version of the world situation in such a blatant manner, but the BBC foreign service was doing a lot to make Americans understand that the British cause was closely linked with the destiny of the United States.

Forty years before, the first transatlantic radio message had been sent without thought as to what it meant. Transmitted from Poldhu, in Cornwall, the three dits of the Morse Code "S" were monitored by Guglielmo Marconi on a pair of earphones at Glace Bay, Newfoundland. It was December 21, 1901, and was historic because the signals were carried through the air. Dots and dashes had gone under the Atlantic through cables as early as fifty years before, but they were limited. This new way of communicating through the air seemed to be almost without limits.

A little over a year later, on January 19, 1903, a message from Theodore Roosevelt to King Edward VII was sent from a Marconi station on Cape Cod, and a reply came back from Cornwall. Morse Code was used again, but this time in words, rather than just a single letter.

Voice transmissions over such a distance did not come until more than a decade later. Leon Trotsky, for instance, used ra-

dio to announce "to all" that the Russian government, in November 1917, was ready to make peace, and his words were
heard all over Europe. The first transatlantic voice transmissions involved French and American amateurs using shortwave sets and occurred about five years later.

In 1924, the British Broadcasting Company aired a speech as
it was being made by the prime minister at the League of Nations in Geneva. It was carried by phone line to London, the
first such international broadcast in Europe. From the United
States, the 1926 Tunney-Dempsey boxing match was broadcast
worldwide, beginning a trend in which a good portion of international broadcasts would concern sports.

All of these news-making events were carried without the direction of network news departments. American radio listeners
could hear news, of a sort—mostly headlines culled from
newspapers. The American networks were not yet in operation
and there were few news programs on individual stations. The
National Broadcasting Company was incorporated on September 9, 1926, and the first broadcast by CBS was two years later.

However, the BBC did establish a news department in 1927,
the same year it became a public corporation, and some of the
procedures used by the BBC in foreign broadcasts were stan-
dard operating procedure by the time American radio men got
to Europe. The BBC news department had three editors and was
supervised by the director of talks, a man who was primarily
responsible for securing people to give radio speeches on topics of public interest.

One of the talkers was Vernon Bartlett. He was known as the
BBC's "foreign correspondent," and for five years, starting in
1927, he gave weekly talks. The series was called "The Way of
the World," and a few of the talks were done from European
capitals where news was being made. After 1932, Bartlett's
continental broadcasts became more frequent, and he could have
claimed—along with several others—the title of first radio foreign correspondent.

The technical arrangements for Bartlett's talks were made from
London in cooperation with the local radio authorities in each
European country. This almost always involved a governmen-
tal agency, since only America had adopted a commercial sys-

tem of broadcasting. Bartlett's main task was to show up at the proper place with script in hand. But sometimes he found his mission was not understood by the local radio officials. "Few broadcast authorities could realize that I was not talking for consumption inside their own frontiers. I was only asking them to give me facilities similar to those given by the ordinary telegraph administration when it transmitted the messages of foreign correspondents to their respective countries."[3]

Bartlett seems to have seen this concern as more of a chamber-of-commerce problem than a political one. "In almost every case the local authorities wanted to censor my talk, and in every case I had to refuse to submit my manuscript in advance. No one in London or abroad seemed able to realize that the maximum of nice things I could say about any country and still retain my British audience was very much smaller than the maximum of nice things the country expected. . . . It was not my job to be indiscriminantly flattering and enthusiastic."[4]

The BBC had rules about what Bartlett was to do. If any official of a foreign country demanded to see the script before he broadcast, Bartlett was to refuse. "Once or twice I had to use that threat and it worked immediately, for the announcement to the British public that the BBC's commentator had not been allowed to express his views about a country would obviously do that country far more harm than if he did express views which were not, in every case, favorable.[5]

To complement the talks by Bartlett and others, BBC chief executive John Reith established a daily newscast in 1927. It was on at 6:30 P.M. Foreshadowing events five years later in America, the proposal to begin a daily newscast on the BBC brought opposition from officials of the newspaper-controlled wire services, who did not want a radio newscast which would cut into the circulation of the British papers. A previous agreement had limited news on the radio to broadcasts after 7 P.M.; morning papers would not be threatened, and by that hour, the evening papers would have been sold.

The first scheduled newscast at 6:30 P.M. contained several "eyewitness descriptions." Whether these were reports by newspapermen working on a free-lance basis or citizens who had witnessed news events is not clear, but there were no BBC reporters as such. The wire services objected in particular to the eyewitness accounts and sought to limit them. In 1930, Reith established a series of "news bulletins" in the evening, beginning at 6 P.M. By that time, the BBC had four editors working in two shifts, and there were also wire service ticker machines in the BBC studios.

There was still room for evolution in the concept of what role objectivity should have in radio news reporting. After leaving the BBC, Bartlett wrote about his perspective.

As a broadcaster I had been a professional optimist. My job had been to take as cheerful a view of affairs as my conscience would allow, because, if I depressed my audience, I should be dismissed. I might try to stimulate them by suggesting how the world could be made better, but I must on no account depress them by suggesting that anything about its organization was fundamentally bad. I was, in fact, becoming a sleek and contented conservative who might arouse supporters of the existing order by a gentle criticism but would never anger them by open attack.[6]

After an uproar over his pro-German statements on the air, Bartlett left the BBC in October 1933 for the *London News Chronicle*, and in 1938 he won a seat in Parliament as an independent progressive.

While transmissions between Britain and the European continent could be made with relative ease, there were a limited number of shortwave stations capable of transmitting a signal from overseas to America. One event which boosted development of shortwave broadcasts internationally was the link between Admiral Byrd's 1929 expedition and a receiving station in Schenectady, New York. Progress reports on the explorers were passed along to the media and made headlines.

The Byrd transmissions were not intended for general use. But the development of shortwave broadcasting by governments and commercial interests, including NBC and CBS, contributed to the establishment of powerful transmitters in world capitals which could carry voices to America for rebroadcast down the network and over the AM frequencies of the local stations.

On February 1, 1929, the first regularly scheduled international shortwave broadcast intended for general consumption was sent from Queen's Hall in London. It was a symphony concert and was clearly heard in the United States, although the broadcast ended before the concert was over. Another pioneering effort was by Marconi, who transmitted a talk from his Chelmsford, England, station to America on December 12, 1929.

The two American networks saw commercial advantages in shortwave broadcasting as they cast their signals toward South America. NBC obtained a shortwave station license in 1929 for a transmitter at Bound Brook, New Jersey, and CBS had a one-kilowatt station. Still, by 1930 there were only five powerful shortwave transmitters in the world. By the eve of World War II, there would be over one hundred.

The Russians were also involved in overseas broadcasts. H. V. Kaltenborn visited Russia in 1930, and heard news being read slowly over the radio. He asked what was going on, and was told that newspaper copy was being transmitted to outlying papers over the airwaves.

French shortwave broadcasts began in 1931, and were aimed at France's overseas possessions. The BBC inaugurated its Empire Service in 1932 with transmissions to Asia, Africa, North and South America, New Zealand, and Australia. Germany followed in 1933 with international broadcasts to America and started broadcasting in foreign languages in 1934. The Italians began international broadcasts in 1935, aimed at the Middle East. In an effort to boost listenership, the Italians gave radios to Arabs who had no receivers, and considering that some may not have had clocks, program times were given in terms of sunrise and sunset.

By 1930, then, it was clear that shortwave broadcasts from Europe to America were feasible. It had also become clear that there was a public appetite for radio news.[7] A partial listing of CBS events carried from Europe in 1930 shows a wide spectrum of program personalities: Bishop Freeman, Albert Einstein, Sir Oswald Mosley, John Masefield, H. G. Wells, and Bill Tilden, all speaking from London. There were about eighty international broadcasts on CBS in 1930. But except for sports coverage, the broadcasts all involved talks by politicians or cultural figures, and not news reports. This pattern for foreign broadcasts would remain until early 1938.

With public interest in overseas developments established and technical ability to provide the broadcasts demonstrated (although there would continue to be problems with the quality of transmission, especially when sunspot activity was high), both networks decided to staff the London Naval Conference in 1930. CBS's man was apparently handpicked by William Paley.[8]

Frederick William Wile was originally a newspaper columnist who had first broadcast on radio in 1923. He had been heard weekly on NBC from 1923 to 1929. The program was called "The Political Situation in Washington Tonight." For the first five years of the broadcast, Wile had not been paid at all, deriving his income from the *Washington Star*. But Wile began to notice that more people were exposed to his ideas on the air than through his column, and he became the first broadcast journalist to strike, demanding fifty dollars a week in 1928. NBC gave Wile the money, but he was stolen away by CBS the next year for an annual salary of $10,000. He became the CBS bureau chief in 1930, and it was that Washington title which he carried to Europe.

NBC sent another Washington commentator to the January 1930 conference. William Hard was known as a "brilliant and fearless commentator on political affairs, with a trenchant, witty style."[9] Max Jordan, who became NBC's first European representative in 1931, says that Hard was such a fine commentator that "none better was ever heard on the American air."[10]

Wile and Hard, strictly speaking, might be called the first American radio foreign correspondents. However, their prime responsibility was to obtain speakers who commented on the proceedings at the conference. Thus, they usually selected men who could speak English well—most often members of the British or American delegations, such as Secretary of State Henry L. Stimson. But Wile and Hard also set the scene for the listeners back in America, introduced the speakers, and reported on developments at the important conference, which was held to determine tonnage limits for fleets of the world powers. CBS scheduled two broadcasts a week from the conference. In one, Wile reviewed the "progress of events." In the other, he introduced a speaker.

The first royal speech ever heard in America was broadcast when King George welcomed the delegates to the conference. Prince Edward, who would later make one of the most famous radio speeches of the decade, also made his American broadcast debut in 1930, during a ship launching.

The man who became CBS's first European representative, Cesar Saerchinger, met Wile during the first week of the conference because they had a mutual friend. Saerchinger stood out because of his size; he was about five feet, three inches tall. At the time of the conference, he was working for an American newspaper chain and had been in Europe since 1918.

Saerchinger invited Wile to go for a Sunday drive in the English countryside, and when Wile said he had to get back to London that afternoon to do a broadcast, Saerchinger asked to go along and have a look at radio foreign correspondence for himself. He describes the facilities Wile used as "what amounted to little more than a telephone booth." But sixty stations carried Wile's reports back in America, and Saerchinger says the broadcasts were "transmitted with startling fidelity." [11]

Twenty-three broadcasts were carried on CBS during the first two months of the conference, although Wile and Hard both returned to Washington before it was over. Saerchinger offered to keep an eye on things for CBS, and because of significant developments, he made a number of broadcasts.

There are some indications that CBS did not plan to continue coverage from Europe after the conference, although Paley claims in his memoirs that "We then decided we wanted someone to stay in London to cover Great Britain and the Continent for us and Saerchinger became that man." [12]

The decision was probably prompted by a telegram Saerchinger sent to New York which read: "Just getting into my stride. Would you be interested in fortnightly series of talks by eminent specialists? Have plan to submit." A cable came back to London asking for details, so Saerchinger sent CBS a year's worth of proposed programs, the final one being George Bernard Shaw "on anything." Three days later the CBS response arrived. "Your plan great. Who speaks Sunday?" [13]

CBS officials must also have polled Wile on Saerchinger's abilities, for Wile takes credit for getting Saerchinger the job, referring to him at one point as "newspaperman Cesar Saerchinger, who, on my recommendation, later became the very able director of CBS activities in Europe."[14]

As Saerchinger writes, his appointment marked the beginning of the American network presence in Europe. "That was the beginning of the first transatlantic broadcast service, and a few weeks later I was the network's officially appointed foreign emissary of radio."[15]

In order to compete with CBS, John Elwood, NBC's foreign relations expert, was sent to Europe in 1931 to find someone to represent the network. Max Jordan, who was just ending a three-year around-the-world cruise and had worked part-time for NBC, was hired by Elwood with this admonishment: "Trans-Atlantic broadcasting is just about to emerge from the experimental stage. It will grow fast from now on. We must be prepared for it."[16]

Jordan had impressive qualifications. He was the product of parents who contributed widely different, but equally important, characteristics to their son. The family was from Wuerttemberg, Germany, and his ancestors were from France and Austria. His mother was a "convinced idealist, always yearned for the good and true no matter where it could be found."[17] His father, a chemist, was ready to go wherever the search might lead. When Max was young, his father ran a drugstore in San Remo, Italy, and then became the Kodak representative for Italy and Switzerland. "Thus, from my boyhood on, I became a traveler. . . . In my formative years my mother never missed an opportunity to instill in my younger brother and myself an appreciation of tolerance and understanding. . . . Having attended school in three different countries, by the time I was in my teens I could carry on in French, German, and sundry dialects. To me the world was vast and beautiful and intriguing."[18]

Jordan received a Ph.D. from Jena University, and joined the staff of the *Berliner Tageblatt* in 1920. Wooed away by the Hearst chain in 1922, he soon became assistant bureau chief in Berlin, and in 1924 he went to New York to be in charge of Hearst's European coverage.

Jordan fell in love with America, and when Hearst officials wanted to send him back to Europe, Jordan quit. He took a job with his old Berlin paper, but this time as Washington correspondent. Jordan got his first glimpse of radio news in 1928 when NBC moved its Washington office across from his in the National Press Building.

As NBC's European representative, Jordan could operate with a thorough knowledge of the continent's geography and languages. He was brought to New York for training, and was given the charge by Elwood: "There is a front page of the air and we need headlines on it 24 hours a day. Go and get some!"[19] Jordan accepted the challenge with anticipation. "There was no limit to one's opportunity. Radiowise, Europe was almost virgin territory. Although broadcasting organizations were in existence in most countries, they could not easily provide for specific American requirements. We had to start from scratch for our own needs."[20]

Just as William L. Shirer would later feel a beginner in competition with Jordan, the relatively seasoned Saerchinger awed Jordan in 1931. There was great rivalry for scoops and much cloak-and-dagger work in order to obtain them. Saerchinger complained that Jordan often led people to believe that his employer, the National Broadcasting Company, was the national network of America. Since European countries almost all had broadcasting systems operated by their governments, NBC's representatives implied a status which did not exist.

Jordan was remembered by an NBC editor who worked with him during the war as "a tall, angular guy, a very quiet man, a very genteel person. He was not aggressive, he was a real good plugger. He was a good, solid newsman."[21]

Both Jordan and Saerchinger used the word "emissary" in describing their jobs. It was likely that they actually saw themselves as representing the American people and helping to provide international understanding. In his selection of speakers for CBS, Saerchinger hoped "The only words they would speak, however fragmentary, might help to heighten our sense of reality, help the ordinary man to form some sort of judgement of their worth."[22]

It seems clear that the network executives thought of their European representatives as procurers, not newsmen. Both Wile and Hard were sent back to Europe to cover the 1932 League of Nations Conference in Geneva. They were joined by Saerchinger and Jordan, and also by Wile's CBS assistant, Shelby Davis, a recent Princeton graduate, and Fred Bate, NBC's new representative in London.

The conference turned out to be overstaffed. So little news developed that after five weeks, all six men departed. While there, says Saerchinger, the radio commentators competed with each other, but not with the newspapers, being "content to parade the voices of eminent statesmen . . . pouring through more or less wishful platitudes."[23]

None of the three men who stayed behind, Jordan, Bate, and Saerchinger, minded that their work primarily involved securing cultural programs for the networks. Bate was not a journalist, having spent most of his time since the end of World War I on the Reparations Committee, which meant that he was familiar with most of the countries of Europe, and the men who ran them. He had worked briefly for a bank prior to accepting the offer from NBC.

In addition to his experience as a print journalist, Saerchinger had an active interest in music. During the previous decade, he had recorded a number of performances and also had done interviews about music in Europe, while living mostly in London. So Saerchinger did not at all question the fact that arranging entertainment programs for broadcast to America was a major part of being the CBS European representative.

Information, instruction, and entertainment are acknowledged to be the principal functions of radio; but the greatest of these by common consent, is entertainment. This at once sums up radio's similarity to journalism, and a vital difference between the two. . . . this distinction determines the present place of broadcasting in the social scheme. It limits its function as a carrier of news, the more so since its basis of measurement is Time, while that of newspapers is Space.[24]

However, CBS had hired two men in 1930 who would come to believe that news was the primary business of the networks' European representatives. Edward Klauber and Paul White were as different as two men could be. But together with Paley they formed a team which made CBS first in news, a lead which was to last for the next half century.

Edward Klauber was born in Louisville, Kentucky, on February 24, 1887. He studied medicine at the University of Louisville and then the University of Pennsylvania, but he left school to become a newspaperman. His uncle was a drama critic at the *New York Times*, and perhaps through his uncle's contacts, Klauber got a job on the *New York World* in 1922. Four years later, he joined the *Times* and became a frequent contributor to the front page. One of his biggest stories was deadline coverage of the mysterious Wall Street bombing of September 16, 1920. In the early years of that decade, Klauber worked on the rewrite desk, and in August 1927 he was promoted to night city editor. Just over a year later, Klauber left the *Times* to become a public relations director of Lennen and Mitchell, Inc., an advertising agency. He would not be a working journalist again during his career, but his obituary in the *Times* makes clear his skill as a writer and editor. "Both as a reporter and rewrite man, Mr. Klauber was known to his colleagues as a perfectionist who took infinite pains with his copy and who regarded newspaper work as deserving of the highest ethical standards. As night city editor, he demanded the same qualities of the staff."[25] Some *Times* staffers found Klauber too demanding. Author Gary Paul Gates says Klauber's "stern manner and exacting demands aroused considerable resentment."[26]

In 1929, Klauber left Lennen and Mitchell to become associated with the Edward L. Bernays public relations organization. The following year, he joined CBS. Paley had nearly rejected Klauber after an initial meeting. He just did not seem like the right man for the job of assistant to the president. But after a second interview, Paley did hire the man from the *Times*.[27]

By the end of 1931, Klauber had become executive vice-president at CBS. The two men complemented each other well. While some may see him as a hatchet man for Paley, his contribution to CBS was greater than that, especially in the area of news. Paley describes their approach in these terms.

Our method was to discuss any given problem until we had exhausted the possibilities and alternatives involved. Once we made a decision we would get it down on paper and that would become a guiding policy for the network. Thus we agreed there would be no editorializing during news broadcasts, commentaries would be kept completely separate from the news itself, CBS news would be accurate and objective.

That was easy enough. But beyond that, we both wanted our radio news and commentaries to achieve a fairness and a balance. If we gave one side of a controversy, we would give equal time to the other side.[28]

Paley says he and Klauber also decided at that time to let the news managers interrupt the network whenever the news merited it. And in hiring newsmen for CBS, preference for good reporting was given over good voice.

It would be truly impressive if Klauber and Paley had decided all of this in 1930. More likely, the principles evolved over several years and were not always strictly followed. There are several instances where the guidelines about interruptions in entertainment programming, and the valuing of good journalism over good vocal chords were bent, if not broken.

However, the tone was set by Paley and Klauber, and in White, CBS had a man who could coordinate news coverage at the high level desired by the CBS executives.

Paul Welrose White was born on June 9, 1902, in Pittsburg, Kansas. His father was a stone contractor. After high school graduation in 1918, White worked for a year on three Midwest newspapers and then started college at the University of Kansas, majoring in journalism. He went to summer school at Colorado University in 1921, and that fall he entered Columbia. A year later he was admitted to the senior class at the Columbia School of Journalism, and he graduated in 1923. While at Columbia, he was a member of the dramatic society, the editorial board for all school publications, and manager of the university debating team. He toured Britain with the debaters and competed against Oxford and Cambridge.

White returned to the journalism school that fall, and in the spring received his master's degree, having written his thesis on "the change in fashions of news as evidenced in the American press since the turn of the century."[29] He had added to his previous newspaper experience by working part-time during the school year, and full-time during the summers.

Upon earning his master's degree, White landed a job with the *New York Evening Bulletin*, and in his first year with the paper he was assigned to cover the Democratic convention. He joined the United Press in August 1924, and reported such major stories of the 1920s as the transatlantic flights of Lindbergh, Byrd, Elder, and Chamberlin-Levine. He was also at times a cable editor, acting sports editor, rewrite man and editor of United Features Syndicate and the United Press mail service. When White joined CBS in December 1930, he came as a news editor in the publicity department. By 1932, he was publicity director. And during the Press Association-radio news war, he operated the newly formed Columbia News Services, Inc.

NBC also had a new man working on news in the early 1930s. Abel A. Schechter was born August 10, 1907, in Central Falls, Rhode Island. He put himself through journalism school at Boston University by working on the *Providence Journal*, and after college he put in brief stints on the *Newark Star Eagle* and *New York World*. Schechter stayed with the *World* for about four years, until it folded, and then moved on to the Associated Press. He soon went to another wire service, INS (International News Service), where he became the youngest city editor it had ever had. But the stay there was also a short one, and by 1932, Schechter was working in the publicity department at NBC. "We had no news department. So I, having probably the most experience with press associations and newspapers, was told that I was the news department." (Interview, April 4, 1981).

Radio news went back to the earliest days of broadcasting, but only in limited quantities. Bill Slocum of the *New York Herald Tribune* had a fifteen-minute news program over WJZ in New York in 1923. Later that year, a young newspaper editor from the *Brooklyn Eagle*, H. V. Kaltenborn, began to broadcast news on WEAF, also a New York station. CBS had started its daily news coverage early in 1929, with a summary lasting five minutes. It was broadcast during a half-hour-long morning show called "Something for Everyone," and was heard on about fifty affiliates.

In December 1929, radio station KFAB in Lincoln, Nebraska, inaugurated what were called "editions of a radio newspaper." The success of the two newscasts each day caused development of similar programs at other local stations. Late in 1930, KMPC in Beverly Hills, California, began to offer three fifteen-minute newscasts daily, and organized the Radio News Service of America, with ten reporters providing information for the broadcasts.

For the most part, though, Americans still relied on newspapers for their news. The local stations tended to get their local news from area papers, and national and international news from the papers or, in some cases, by subscribing to the wire services. On the basis of one United Press teletype machine in its newsroom, CBS claimed to be the top news network in April 1931. This claim meant that CBS had interrupted regular commercial programs with UP bulletins more frequently than NBC. CBS press releases were headed "Columbia—the News Network." [30] Not mentioned was the fact that NBC had more popular programs and perhaps more to lose by interruptions.

In an effort to obtain more bulletins for CBS, the man in charge of the news, Director of Publicity Jesse S. Butcher, had requested more service from UP, particularly in the evening, when radio had its largest audience. At the time, CBS was not paying for the wire; credit was given to the UP every time a bulletin from it was read.

However, the Press-Radio War, which ran from 1931 to 1934, stopped the networks from obtaining wire service copy for several years and, more importantly, caused the development of news departments at both NBC and CBS. The battle was led on one side by the Associated Press, which was a cooperative venture of its member newspapers. At their annual meeting in 1931, prodded by those belonging to the AP, the members of the American Newspaper Publishers Association passed a resolution calling for newspaper control of radio news.

The newspaper owners were uneasy about the increasing competition from radio. In March 1932, CBS had beaten the newspapers on the Lindbergh kidnapping, with most of its advantage won by Boake Carter, a Philadelphia broadcaster who went on to gain national prominence as a commentator. NBC had delayed broadcasting the story until the newspapers could get extra editions on the streets.

The networks also obtained large audiences for their coverage of the 1932 national conventions. In reaction, the directors of the Associated Press voted to deny the networks use of election returns that year. But when Kent Cooper, the powerful general manager of the AP, found out that CBS was planning to buy United Press election news for $1,000, he wavered. Cooper did not want millions of Americans to hear the results of the election on CBS with credit for the results going to UP. Negotiations went down to the last few days before the election.

At the same time, Karl Bickel, the president of UP, was being pressured by his service's clients to rescind the agreement with CBS, which he did. But Cooper did not know that and agreed to provide AP results for CBS. Realizing that the shoe was now on the other foot, someone at UP ordered the teletype in the CBS newsroom, which had been idle until then, turned on. And finally, INS also installed a teletype machine as the night wore on, giving CBS, in the end, results from all three wire services.

Despite the last-minute developments, CBS would have had the results anyway. It had made arrangements with the *New York Times* and the *New York Journal* to receive returns, including those of at least two, and perhaps all three, of the wire services to which the papers subscribed. The CBS election coverage was anchored by Frederick William Wile and Edwin C. Hill. NBC had Walter Lippmann, George B. Parker, and Arthur Brisbane.

When the winner of the election, Franklin D. Roosevelt, was inaugurated on March 4, 1933, not only did millions of Americans listen in, but so did millions of foreigners on an international feed. More importantly for the growth of radio, President Roosevelt would use the medium eight days later for his first fireside chat. The new leader understood the power radio could generate and became a master at using it. And radio, in turn, benefitted from the Presidential seal of approval.

While UP and INS continued to sell news to broadcasters, AP would not. At the April 1933 AP members' convention, a resolution was passed which specifically denied AP news to the networks. Pressure was applied by powerful clients of UP and INS to follow AP's lead. CBS responded by setting up a news service with Paul White as vice-president and general manager. The main office was, of course, in New York with bureaus in Los Angeles and Chicago. White already had Wile in Washington and Saerchinger in London. Eight hundred stringers were signed up. CBS obtained international news from the British

Exchange Telegraph and the Central News Agency, and finan-
cial news from the Dow Jones wire.

White hired as his assistant a thirty-six-year-old reporter for
the *New York Herald Tribune*, Edward Angley. A former foreign
correspondent for the AP in London, Paris, Berlin, and Moscow, Angley was in charge of gathering and writing most of
the news, which included reports from men at CBS affiliates
across the country. Angley was also a free-lance writer during
this time, returning to the *Herald Tribune* in 1936, and eventually going back to foreign correspondence in 1936 as the paper's London bureau chief. By September 1933, CBS was offering two fifteen-minute newscasts a day, with Boake Carter and
H. V. Kaltenborn as the readers.

NBC had done less about gathering the news, but Schechter
found that a telephone and the prestige of NBC could make up
for a lack of stringers. Nearly everyone in America, save the
President, would answer a call from NBC, especially when it
was made known that the call was being made on behalf of
popular newsman Lowell Thomas. And in order to augment
their coverage, NBC arranged to receive bulletins from Consol-
idated News.

Dealing from a position of relative strength, David Sarnoff of
NBC's parent company, RCA, NBC President M. H. Ayles-
worth, and CBS's Paley decided in November 1933 to seek a
peace treaty. Negotiations did not last long; and in December,
an agreement was reached between the networks and representatives of the National Association of Broadcasters on one
side, and the heads of AP, UP, INS, and several major newspapers on the other.

The newspapers wanted limits similar to those proposed for
the BBC in Britain: only brief items to be supplied by the wire
services, and no bulletins before the morning and afternoon
papers had hit the streets. The broadcasters wanted to ensure
their right to broadcast news as soon as they got it.

The "Biltmore agreement" reached between radio and print
officials gave most of the advantage to the new medium. The
networks and stations were to stop gathering news on their own.
A new Press-Radio Bureau would use the wire service copy to
compile two summaries each day, which, when read on the air,

would last about five minutes. They were to be broadcast at 9:30
A.M. and 9 P.M. and would not be sponsored. However, radio
newsrooms were allowed to receive bulletins of "transcendent
importance," and these could be read immediately. By the time
the agreement went into effect in March 1934, most news was
being sent to the networks as bulletins.

The day before the new bureau was to begin sending news
to the networks and radio stations that subscribed, a compet-
ing service started selling news. It was a cooperative, with twenty
stations as members, but after three weeks it was abandoned.
Most of its members had been from the West, and the stations
from the East did not want most of the news offered to them.

But on March 21, 1934, a second service was offered by the
same people who managed the failed effort. Called the Transradio Press Service, it had bureaus in America's major cities and
such powerful stations as KNX in Hollywood and and KSTP in
St. Paul were clients. Most of the news was supplied by stringers, claimed to number seven thousand, but Transradio also offered news from Havas of France, and later from Reuter.

By the end of 1934, Transradio had 150 clients who paid between 5 and 500 dollars a week. The least amount of copy received was 5,000 words a week, sent by cable to save expense,
and a station could arrange to have six times that much. In August 1934, Transradio started up an auxiliary service featuring
two improvements. Radio News Association copy was transmitted by shortwave. And it was written in more of a broadcast
style than the regular Transradio copy.

Other radio news agencies also were formed in competition
with the Press-Radio Bureau, but none was as successful as
Transradio. UP and AP executives saw the inroads being made
and decided they had to be competitive. They offered their copy
to radio outlets, and pushed back the window for broadcast news
to 8 A.M. and 6 P.M. In return, the networks agreed to stop their
independent news gathering, and to rely on the bureau for news.
Looking back, Paley wondered about the price the networks paid
for peace with the print media.[31]

While the networks in America were making their first significant steps into news gathering, the competition for foreign
broadcasts also escalated. Saerchinger had Europe pretty much

to himself from the time of his appointment as CBS European representative in early 1930 until the end of that year. NBC used intermediaries, such as the manager of European operations for one of the wire services. This arrangement was not viable, as competition between the two networks over a talk by Mahatma Gandhi illustrates. The Indian pacifist was in Europe to promote the cause of independence for his homeland, and both networks very much wanted to bring his voice to American listeners. At first it seemed that Gandhi would appear just on NBC. However, because some CBS affiliates also belonged to the press association, pressure was put on the NBC intermediary, and Gandhi ended up on both networks.

The first election results broadcast from Europe were those of the British general election in 1931. Saerchinger was in New York on his annual vacation, and while he contributed from America, the anchoring in England was done by the BBC's Raymond Gram Swing.

Often, the place of origin or the notoriety of the speaker counted more heavily than the content of the talk. On New Year's Day, 1931, Mussolini made his first (and last) radio speech in English, having practiced with a tutor for some time. Intimates had told him his English was excellent, but when it came time to broadcast, few American listeners could understand the Italian's English.

And even though there were many more native-speaking Germans in the United States in 1931 than there are now, it is difficult to understand the benefit of carrying a speech entirely in German, which is what CBS did when General Paul von Hindenburg spoke in the fall of that year.

With few exceptions, all international broadcasts were coming from Europe in the early 1930s, and the reasons would have great impact on foreign correspondence in the future. For one thing, most of the world's powerful shortwave transmitters were there, the BBC facilities being especially good. And most of the world's powers were there, at least as perceived by political leaders in the Western world. Third, the majority of Americans were culturally linked to Europe. For these reasons, the bulk of international print news as well was focused on Europe and the colonies of the European countries, and the news in the papers influenced what was carried on radio.

However, one of the exceptions foreshadowed events of a decade later. In January 1932, Floyd Gibbons, a veteran foreign correspondent for newpapers, sent a radio report from the Manchurian war zone where Japan was advancing against China. Guns could be heard in the background. NBC augmented that report with broadcasts from China on the fall of Shanghai and Nanjing, and the bombing of the U.S. Navy gunboat, *Panay*. These reports were strictly on a stringer basis. In Japan, listeners to NHK heard reports from China from reporters for the national network who were sent to the front.

The Soviet Union was linked to America in 1933 when Jordan arranged for a conversation between the Soviet commissar for foreign affairs and his wife to be broadcast. Maxim Litvinov was in Washington at the time of the December 16 broadcast, and his wife was in Moscow. Jordan reports that Mrs. Litvinov came through "clear as a bell," although he adds that it was the first and last broadcast from Russia that was not censored.

The most extensive news report on the air anywhere in the world in the early 1930s was probably that of the BBC. The "News Reel" had been started in 1919 and ran fifty minutes. It featured live switches to such places as Manchester and Paris, and also contained elements recorded on gramophones and Blattnerphones, the latter a cylindrical forerunner of the tape recorder. It was very popular, but the broadcast was taken off the air in December 1933 because it was also very expensive to produce.

The BBC staff was expanded in 1934, and in addition, a separate news department was set up in the Empire and Foreign Services branch. This allowed increased foreign coverage, although "News Reel" did not return until the war started, and then only on the Empire Service.

Despite the increased staff and coverage, the BBC did not have a full-time foreign correspondent until 1939. And the BBC announcers were not averse to announcing, particularly at the hour scheduled for a brief evening update, "Owing to a lack of events, there is no news tonight."[32] In contrast to the disintegration of the press-radio agreement in America, the BBC was still limited to giving news between 6 P.M. and 2 A.M., and only 400 eyewitness accounts could be used each year.

But in the United States, the amount of news offered listeners seems paltry by today's standards. NBC had two networks, the Red and the Blue. On the Red, there was no news at all; on the Blue, there was Lowell Thomas. CBS offered the brief reports of Boake Carter and Edwin C. Hill, and mostly in fringe time, the commentaries of H. V. Kaltenborn and others, which sometimes contained news. Sponsors generally did not want news programs, and the few who did expected veto power over the content of the broadcasts.

The Mutual Radio Network was founded in September 1934, and Johnny Johnstone was appointed news director, but Mutual had little impact on the development of broadcast foreign correspondence. It relied almost totally on stringers until 1938, when former *Chicago Tribune* correspondent John Steele was made London representative.

If veto power over programming seems a violation of ethical standards, there were other practices of dubious value. Jordan tells of taking the *Graf Zeppelin* to Brazil and Chicago in 1933, and of being the first to report to the public from an airship in flight to the Americas. He went as a guest of the public relations agency which represented the owners of the aircraft.

While most of the talks heard in America were done free or for a nominal fee, desire to have exclusivity generated bidding wars at times. Saerchinger wrote about one case in which CBS was outbid by NBC. "The result was that the broadcast cost hundreds more than it should. Competition still keeps the pots (other people's) boiling." [33]

Leon Trotsky gave a talk from Copenhagen in November 1932 and received compensation. At first, he asked for a lot of money, but for some reason—perhaps a desire for exposure—his request was reduced to such a small sum that Saerchinger said any American crooner would consider it low.

NBC scored a beat of sorts in broadcasting Hitler's first speech after his election. CBS had an opportunity to buy it, but when Hitler proposed a $1,500 fee for the fifteen-minute talk, network officials in New York cabled Saerchinger: "Unwant Hitler Any Price." What NBC got for its money hardly seems worth the price paid. The talk was in German, and Jordan had to give a hushed simultaneous translation. Later Hitler speeches were not carried at all, reports Jordan, because they were too boring.

The desire to provide exciting broadcasts may have caused some events to be staged. While doing a broadcast on the Saar plebiscite, Saerchinger wanted celebrating citizens to be heard in the background. He had made arrangements for a group of local people to gather under the window of the room from which he was broadcasting, but they missed the cue, and Saerchinger had to send an engineer to a nearby bar to fetch them. Once they arrived, the broadcaster helped out by shouting down titles of songs he wanted them to sing.

There were also problems in these early days of foreign correspondence which had nothing to do with the equipment. Vernon Bartlett recalled one broadcast which was ruined when two technicians got into a heated argument and knocked against a control-room knob, which put him off the air.

In some countries, the national broadcasting system officials did not put much value on punctuality, and broadcasts might be started late or be allowed to run past the scheduled termination. On more than one occasion, the network representatives sent out what they thought was a brilliant broadcast, only to find the next day that it had been lost somewhere in space or was not even transmitted.

Some of the programs which were sent to America from Europe were of questionable value. A CBS broadcast from England of a nightingale singing for thirty minutes was voted the most interesting program of the year by newspapermen who edited radio pages in American newspapers. The first foreign man-on-the-street interviews to be heard in America were done by H. V. Kaltenborn in Picadilly Circus. It was part of his CBS coverage of the London Economic Conference in June 1933.

One year and one month later, a more reliable indication of the future of broadcasting occurred in Austria. During the Nazi Putsch on July 25, 1934, the first target was the Federal Chancery, with Chancellor Engelbert Dollfuss inside. The second was, however, the Ravag, Austria's broadcast center. A technician cut the cable to the transmitter before the Nazis could broadcast, but Saerchinger noted: "The important fact is that in this attempted revolution the broadcast headquarters was deemed a primary point of attack and so it will be in all revolutions from now on."[34]

Jordan had already looked at the Nazi agenda and decided he needed to base his operations in Switzerland. The move from Berlin to Basel would give him more journalistic mobility—physically and philosophically. A further hint of trouble came in September 1935, when Emporer Haile Selassie broadcast an appeal to the world for intervention in Ethiopia. Mussolini responded several weeks later with a warlike challenge from Rome, and both speeches were carried by NBC and CBS.

The European representatives were being stretched to their limits by an increasing demand for programs. Saerchinger complained. "I was expected to cover not merely England, but all of Europe single-handed and to land every dictator and 'stuff shirt' making front page headlines in the American press."[35]

Still, when President Roosevelt went to South America in 1936, Saerchinger was instructed by White to limit European material, and Saerchinger felt left out. The feeling did not last long. The Berlin Olympics in 1936 gave the Germans an opportunity to display their technical excellence, and they provided an elaborate facility for broadcasters. The networks took advantage of it; NBC, for instance, sent seventy-five reports back to the United States during the games. But the Spanish Civil War caught Saerchinger in Berlin when he needed to be near Spain, and one man truly was unable to cover the quickly escalating situation in Europe.

Saerchinger was forced to send his "Paris man, Didier van Ackere," to Hendaye, France, to cover the war from just over the border. However, H. V. Kaltenborn was on another of his self-proclaimed fact-finding tours of Europe, and White sent him a cable in Paris. Kaltenborn traveled south to Hendaye and made several broadcasts. But the one which will be remembered came a week later, on September 7, 1936.

The first foreign correspondents to arrive in Hendaye, not far across the border from Irún, had located a cafe which overlooked the battlefield on the other side of the border. They would sit there and sip drinks while "covering" the war. The terrain was such that boundaries followed a riverbed with Spanish territory on either side of a French peninsula. The farmers who lived on the French finger had departed at the suggestion of authorities, but Kaltenborn and his French technician found a phone in working order in an abandoned farmhouse.

The phone was tapped, and the bold technician ran a line out of a haystack in an open field. A complicated circuit was arranged via Paris and London to a British shortwave transmitter at Rugby. That turned out to be the easy part. When Kaltenborn got through to New York to ask for air time, he was told the network had too many commercials to run then and was asked to stand by. Several times bullets cut the line, but the engineer crawled out to patch it. Once New York did give the go-ahead, but an engineer at a relay point in Bordeaux was out for a drink, and the circuit could not be completed. Finally, at 9 P.M., after a six-hour wait, Kaltenborn broadcast for fifteen minutes. The sounds of battle were clearly heard, and never one to be shy about his accomplishments, Kaltenborn declared he had made "the first actual battlefield broadcast on radio history."[36]

The report did get Kaltenborn's name on the front pages of American papers, and won him the Headliner's Club Award. That Saerchinger may have begun to be out of step with the direction broadcasting was taking is revealed in his thoughts about Kaltenborn's broadcast. "The idea of broadcasting a 'running commentary' on the cruelest kind of war, just as you do a football game, was grotesque but perfectly feasible, though the opportunity is not likely to occur again."[37]

Further broadcast reports on the Spanish Civil War were limited. One problem was that there was only one powerful shortwave station in Spain. A Spanish journalist who worked for the BBC did one report for CBS, but censorship was so heavy that Saerchinger found the only value in the report was its place of origin. Floyd Gibbons, ever the war correspondent, did make one uncensored broadcast, and Kaltenborn later did several reports from a small transmitter located in a basement. Spain was not the testing ground for broadcast correspondents that it was for the military men of some of the world powers.

Back in New York, however, Paul White was breaking new ground. He mastered the technical aspects of broadcasting, often running the controls himself, punching up phone connections to bring in reports from the field. CBS was providing scheduled news three times a day during most of 1936: five minutes at noon and 4:30 P.M. and fifteen minutes at 11 P.M. White had a new title, that of director of public events and special fea-

tures. In a press release put out by CBS in September 1936, it
was crowed that:

Anything of interst that happens in the wide world is grist to Columbia's Special Events mill—and Paul White is the man who transfers
the event to radio existence.
The kind of job he has calls for extensive and amazingly varied requirements. He must not only understand completely the technical aspects of radio, he must also be a showman, skilled in the knowledge
of what appeals in the world of entertainment. He must be a diplomat, sensitive to a variety of national and international situations,
shrewd in contacting and winning the good-will of high officials.[38]

White had lived up to at least some of these accolades. During a hurricane disaster in Florida, White wanted to set up a
program from the Miami affiliate. The phone lines were down,
planes could not fly there, and no cables could be sent directly.
So White sent a cablegram via London, Johannesburg, Rio de
Janeiro, and Havana. From Cuba, the message was shortwaved
to Miami, and the program was broadcast as White desired.

One indication of the increasing interest in news on radio came
from a small book published by NBC in early 1937. Like the
glossy promotional books put out by CBS, *35 Hours a Day* pointed
out the accomplishments of the network. In 1936, NBC had offered 590 hours of broadcasts of special news events and current news topics, a figure which represented just 3 percent of
NBC's total programming on its two networks.

About forty of those broadcasts came during a ten-day period in December. The abdication of Great Britain's King Edward VIII was more fully reported in America than it was in
Britain. Strict media controls kept the British press and radio
from reporting much detail of the crisis, but American listeners
heard every development, often from British broadcasters who
could not be heard in their own country on the topic. They included Vernon Bartlett, Stephen King-Hall, and Gerald Barry.

CBS carried thirty-nine broadcasts, which usually ran fifteen
minutes, during the constitutional crisis. But NBC had the advantage because Bate was a member of the king's social circle
and was privy to inside information. The pressure on Saerchinger to produce new details daily was immense. "New York was

never satisfied. When we offered a prominent MP, they wanted Winston Churchill; when we proposed Lord Beaverbrook, they wanted Lord Rothermere as well; when we delivered a viscount, they wanted an earl or a duke. Hardly had we given the latest available news in a midnight talk, when they wanted another one at 4 A.M.—even if there were nothing new! The public was wild and we were going mad. New York rang up to confirm every wild rumor; conservative but reliable information merely aroused a suspicion that I was 'slow.' "[39]

When the king announced his abdication on December 10, Saerchinger capped his coverage with a world scoop. The official announcement was to be made in the House of Commons by the prime minister. The king's famous "Woman I Love" speech would not be made from Windsor Castle until the next day. Every reporter gathered at the House of Commons was searching for some sign of what was going to happen. But Saerchinger had astutely posted a "scout" near the House of Lords, where the announcement was made first, with the press barred. When his tipster signalled that the king had stepped aside, Saerchinger had only a moment before he was to turn the broadcast line over to the prime minister. He introduced the speaker with these words: "The King has abdicated. Here is Sir Frederick Whyte to speak to you about this momentous event."[40] The CBS exclusive held for twenty minutes, until the wire services could transmit the facts to America. When His Royal Highness talked to the world on December 11, it was as former king that he attracted the largest audience in the world ever to hear a speech.

On the whole, however, the number of programs carrying headline news from overseas to America were few compared to the ones which were only for purposes of entertainment or which contained familiar banalities. Saerchinger recognized the need for a change: "radio organizations should treat these pre-fabricated broadcasts as the newspapers treat so called handouts— pick out the 'raisins' and look for the holes. The time has come, too, for the elimination of the world wide engineering stunts by which statesmen in a dozen countries repeat, one after the other, sublime platitudes about peace. . . . In 1932 it was an impressive novelty; today it is a bore."[41]

A memo drawn up at CBS about 1936 reveals that White and Klauber were planning to change some of the practices which had irritated Saerchinger. The plan was to cut down on unnecessary hook-ups, fictitious enthusiasm, and maudlin sentimentality. The news executives also wanted to find qualified journalists to augment the CBS domestic staff.

CBS officials were also interested in obtaining more news from overseas, but did not want to use the voice of its European representative. Saerchinger was expected to secure the services of newsmen from the wire services, newspapers, and foreign broadcasting systems.

Although events in Europe caused more reports from overseas to be brought to American listeners, CBS officials were not yet thinking about getting a newsman to replace Saerchinger. But they were thinking about a replacement. The criticism from New York during the British constitutional crisis indicates that Paley, Klauber, and White felt Saerchinger may have been slowing down, or lacked the contacts necessary to provide superior coverage. He had turned forty-six in October 1936, but was not appreciably older than his rivals at NBC. Another factor against Saerchinger may have been his devotion to music, although entertainment programs, including musical ones, would continue to be an important part of the new representative's bailiwick.

The new CBS man in London was Edward R. Murrow, who had been hired in 1935 as director of talks. The new twenty-seven-year-old employee was the subject of a memo shortly after Paley met Murrow for the first time. Finding Murrow to be a "sober, earnest young man," Paley had suggested to Klauber that they might have found the best man to head all of CBS's international broadcasting.[42]

But the offer from Klauber to Murrow did not come until many months later—February 1937. The only reason Paley gives for the change is hardly a full explanation. "We needed such a man, for our broadcasts from Europe were on the rise."[43] Murrow did have some impressive credentials but not as a broadcaster. After attending three colleges and graduating Phi Beta Kappa from Washington State University in 1930, Murrow had served as president of the National Student Federation with a weekly stipend of twenty-five dollars. He had been elected after making a speech charging that American students were "too provincial, overly concerned with fraternities, football, and fun, and too unconcerned with the wider world."[44]

Murrow had been through most of the western United States during stints as a surveyor in Alaska, British Columbia, and Washington. His first trip to Europe came while president of the NSFA in 1930, when he went to a meeting of an international student federation in Brussels. The trip lasted only a couple of weeks. Although he did manage to stop in Britain, he was not much impressed by it, especially the rainy weather.

In the summer of 1931, Murrow went to Europe again, driving with friends from France to Hungary, where another student conference was being held. He was dismayed by the effect nationalism was having on the delegations. After it was over, he went on to Turkey before returning home.

Murrow stepped down from his post with the NSFA, only to take a job as assistant director of the Institute of International Education, which was closely associated with his former student group. He had added two years to his real age on the application, which seemed hardly necessary since the director was well acquainted with Murrow.[45]

His new job meant Murrow attended student conventions again, but his duties also included arranging speeches by academics, including some radio broadcasts. Murrow wrote a book with James T. Shotwell, *Channels of International Cooperation*; it is one of the few pieces of print journalism he ever did.

Murrow also did some broadcasting as part of his job. CBS had apparently approached him about doing a number of broadcasts on education, but one of the two parties did not follow through. The next year, 1934, Murrow did several more radio talks, including one on CBS about the relationship between education and democracy. He enjoyed the experience and vowed to do more broadcasting in the future.

But Murrow's most important public statement that year was "I do." He and Janet Brewster, two years his junior, were married October 27, 1934, in Middletown, Connecticut. They had attended a number of the same student conferences when she was a student at Mount Holyoke College, and he was one of

the leaders of the organizations. Their honeymoon included stops
at his birthplace in Polecat Creek, North Carolina, in Mexico and
at his parents' house in Washington state. Then the Murrows
returned to New York to live in an apartment in the east six-
ties.

Ed Murrow was making $5,000 a year with the Institute and
devoting much of his energy to the Emergency Committee in
Aid of Displaced German Scholars, an effort which would result in relocation for over 300 academicians who had fled the
Nazis. He learned about the opening at CBS from Fred Willis,
an assistant to Paley and also director of education for the network. Willis and Murrow had known each other initially through
the international student movement, and later as both became
involved in educational broadcasts.

In the summer of 1935, the newly created position of director
of talks at CBS had first been given to Raymond Gram Swing,
a commentator known to both American and European audiences. But when Swing found the director would only arrange
for speakers and not broadcast himself, he backed out. Klauber
offered the position to Murrow, and he accepted it with the understanding that he could finish his work for the Institute, and
while doing that, take his wife to Europe. They worked their
way across the Atlantic as social directors on a Dutch liner. In
England, they met Cesar Saerchinger for the first time and went
to France, Germany, and Holland, with Murrow attending to
Institute business here and there.

Searchinger would now have two bosses: one of them was
White and the new one, Murrow. He did not seem to mind—
he was the only full-time representative CBS had overseas, and
he handled the requests as they came. Arranging a speech by
a politician was more or less the same as setting up the broadcast of a concert.

CBS had overtaken NBC in number of affiliates by the end of
1935, offering network programs on more than 100 of them.
Despite rapid growth, there was still a feeling of discovery among
the employees at CBS and a striving for excellence in all parts
of the company. About the same time Murrow was hired, Frank
Stanton joined CBS as a researcher making fifty-five dollars a
week. Within a decade he would be president of the network.

Another man who joined CBS at the same time, Jules Dundes, found the stimulating atmosphere spread to all parts of the company. "You had the feeling that this was new, was burgeoning, there was lots of growth to be encountered. It was a glamorous and exciting kind of thing. Family and friends were quite impressed that you worked for an outfit like CBS."[46] Dundes worked for the promotion department, and his supervisors included Vic Ratner and Paul Keston. Their idea was to promote the idea of radio in general, so CBS would benefit from the enhancement of the medium in the public's eyes. The department was small but the product was of high quality. "The others, like NBC, could do nothing but copy. CBS was so good. . . . Basically it can be expressed this way—Keston said it more than once: 'We are in the advertising business. It is our responsibility therefore, to be better at advertising than all the people to whom we want to sell our time.' So it was his premise that when we put something on paper it had to be superb, and it was."[47]

A floor or two below the promotion department, the director of public events and special features was technically in charge of the director of talks. Between White and Murrow there developed a rivalry which at times became less than friendly, and it continued into later years when Murrow was in Europe, and also after the war when Murrow became White's boss.[48]

Murrow did make his broadcast debut as a CBS employee before leaving for Europe. Robert Trout, one of the central CBS newscasters, had gone to a publicity department Christmas party which went on into the evening. Nearly thirty years later, during a 1964 broadcast, both men enjoyed a laugh over what happened when Trout and Murrow left the party.

Trout: I was practically a teetotaller; I didn't know anything about this alcohol, and you were always very circumspect. And as the evening wore on, I remembered I had to do a five-minute newscast, supplied by the Press-Radio Bureau. You decided that I really wasn't quite fit to do it. Do you remember that?

Murrow: If this is being recorded, I don't remember anything about it.

Trout: And I sat in the studio when I was supposed to be doing it, and you did it.

Murrow: That's right. And you were going to give me the cut, you were
going to give me the watch at the end, and you gave it to me a
minute early, and we left fourty-five seconds of dead air at the
end.[49]

Although shorter than expected, the broadcast was apparently well delivered. And neither man was rebuked for what
had happened.[50]

NOTES

1. Joseph J. Mathews, *Reporting the Wars* (Westport, Conn.: Greenwood, 1957), p. 54.
2. Abel A. Schechter, *Go Ahead Garrison!: A Story of News Broadcasting* (New York: Dodd, Mead, 1940), p. 199.
3. Vernon Bartlett, *Intermission in Europe—the Life of a Journalist and
Broadcaster* (New York: Oxford University Press, 1938), p. 136.
4. Ibid., p. 135.
5. Ibid., p. 143.
6. Ibid.
7. An audience estimated at sixty-three million had tuned into CBS
and NBC coverage of President Hoover's inauguration in March 1929.
William S. Paley, *As It Happened: A Memoir* (Garden City, N.Y.: Doubleday, 1979), p. 118.
8. Ibid., p. 12l.
9. Cesar Saerchinger, *Hello America—Radio Adventures in Europe*
(Boston: Houghton, Mifflin, 1938), p. 4.
10. Max Jordan, *Beyond All Fronts* (Milwaukee: Bruce, 1944), p. 50.
11. Saerchinger, *Hello America*, p. 4.
12. Paley, *As It Happened*, p. 120.
13. Saerchinger, *Hello America*, p. 11.
14. Frederick William Wile, *News Is Where You Find It* (New York:
Bobbs-Merrill, 1939), p. 443.
15. Saerchinger, *Hello America*, p. 11.
16. Jordan, *Beyond All Fronts*, p. 29.
17. Ibid., p. 4.
18. Ibid., pp. 4, 5, and 29.
19. This may have been inspirational to Jordan, but it hardly reflected reality. Neither network was broadcasting twenty-four hours a
day then. For short periods, as war became imminent, NBC and CBS

did stay on the air around the clock. But the first regular twenty-four-hour service did not start until the early 1970s on CBS.

Second, many of the broadcasts Jordan was asked to arrange were not headline material. They included such non-events as academic lectures and performing animals.

20. Jordan, *Beyond All Fronts*, p. 45.

21. Burroughs Prince, former night news editor for NBC, interview with the author, January 27, 1981.

22. Saerchinger, *Hello America*, p. 93.

23. Ibid., p. 178.

24. Ibid., p. 177.

25. *New York Times*, September 24, 1954, p. 23.

26. Gary Paul Gates, *Air Time—the Inside Story of CBS News* (New York: Harper & Row, 1978), p. 98.

27. Paley, *As It Happened*, p. 63.

28. Ibid., p. 120.

29. From the CBS Research Library files. Press releases dated 9/3/36 and 8/17/37.

30. Paley, *As It Happened*, p. 122.

31. Ibid., p. 129.

32. Barton Paulu, *British Broadcasting* (Minneapolis: University of Minnesota Press, 1956), pp. 155–57.

33. Saerchinger, *Hello America*, p. 148.

34. Ibid., p. 204.

35. Ibid., p. 79.

36. H. V. Kaltenborn, Columbia University Oral History, p. 19l. Gibbons's report from Manchuria also featured the sounds of war. The argument is one of proximity.

37. Saerchinger, *Hello America*, p. 225.

38. CBS Research Library. CBS press release dated 9/3/36.

39. Saerchinger, *Hello America*, p. 237.

40. Alexander Kendrick, *Prime Time* (Boston: Little, Brown, 1969), p. 143.

41. Saerchinger, *Hello America*, p. 112.

42. Paley, *As It Happened*, p. 13l.

43. Ibid.

44. Kendrick, *Prime Time*, p. 110.

45. Ibid., p. 117. Murrow had a propensity for enhancing certain facts on his resume. He would later add several more years to his age in applying at CBS, and also changed specifics about his education. This caused confusion later on, including incorrect information in his obit-

uary in the *New York Times*. Murrow had previously stopped calling himself by his given name, Egbert, after graduating from high school. See David Holbrook Culbert, *News for Everyman: Radio and Foreign Affairs in Thirties America* (Westport, Conn.: Greenwood 1976), p. 183; and Kendrick, *Prime Time*, p. 98.

46. Jules Dundes, interview with the author, September 24, 1980. Dundes went on to a career with CBS that lasted more than thirty years, and included a radio network vice-presidency. He is now a lecturer in the Communications Department at Stanford University and director of its Summer Broadcast Institute.

47. Ibid.

48. As vice-president for news and public affairs, Murrow fired White in 1946. CBS was starting a new fifteen-minute long evening newscast under the 1.5 million dollar sponsorship of the Campbell Soup Company. White was to introduce Robert Trout, anchorman of "The World Today." According to Eric Sevareid, "White went on drunk and it sounded like it, and Ed went down the elevator and fired him immediately, to everybody's astonishment." (Interview with the author, November 6, 1980.) Kendrick says Murrow did not find White in the studio, that White had already left the building. Kendrick states the official version was that White left as part of the "network reconversion program." (Kendrick, *Prime Time*, p. 294.) Print accounts (*New York Times*, July 10, 1955, and others) give the reason for departure as White's desire to write a book, which turned out to be *News on the Air*. He did suffer from arthritis, and "illness" was given by the *Times* as his reason for moving to San Diego in 1947.

49. CBS Radio Network, "Farewell to Studio Nine," July 26, 1964.

50. Kendrick, *Prime Time*, p. 137. The version of the incident in *Prime Time* may be a case where the legend grew over time, while some of the facts were blurred.

2 · Preparing for a Chance

When the Murrows sailed for England in April 1937, Ed Murrow went as a procurer of talks and entertainment, not as a talker himself. Trout and White followed on the next ship because a new king was to be crowned in London, and Trout was to introduce the six BBC announcers who did most of CBS's broadcast. It lasted six hours. The Murrows were spectators, watching the procession pass by Hyde Park corner.

In addition to being carried on the CBS network, the feed from London was also sent to Latin America on Columbia's new shortwave station, W2XE. Trout and White did not return to New York until June 10, 1937, having done several other broadcasts from Europe over the two-month period. They were not hard news programs, but such things as a broadcast from Le Bourget Field in France commemorating the tenth anniversary of Charles Lindbergh's landing there, and one from London in which Trout gave his impressions of the city.

Saerchinger turned over the CBS offices in Langham Place, across from the Broadcasting House of the BBC, and returned to America. He would appear again on U.S. radio programs, but this time from New York. In 1940 he was on NBC weekly with a broadcast called "Stories behind the Headlines." He turned more toward print after that, publishing *The Way out of War* and other books.

Some of the first broadcasts the new European director arranged from Britain showed Murrow's desire to keep radio in tune with the common man. He did a series of broadcasts on Saturday nights from a public house in which the voices of

working people were heard. And on occasion, Murrow's voice
was heard too. One of his first broadcasts from Europe was a
description of the 1937 Boy Scout World Jamboree in the Netherlands. A later program that year concerned Murrow doing a
man-on-the-street interview from the English seaside resort of
Brighton during a national holiday. In December, he read a
translation of Haile Selassie's Christmas message.

Within a few months of his arrival in London, Murrow sought
a continental assistant. NBC had Bate in London and Jordan in
Switzerland. William L. Shirer may have first come to the attention of White and Murrow when he did a report from Berlin
on May 7, 1937. White was still in Europe then, and Saerchinger was probably still in charge of the London office. Shirer had
received a phone call from Claire Trask, who had helped Saerchinger monitor events in Germany and, on a part-time basis,
arranged for speakers for the network. Trask wanted Shirer to
do a broadcast on German reaction to the Hindenberg dirigible
disaster. Shirer was working full-time in the Berlin bureau of
the Universal News Service.

Several hours before, on what was May 6 in America, the huge
airship exploded as it was attempting to tie up at Lakehurst,
New Jersey. Herbert Morrison of WLS in Chicago was describing the scene into a microphone—not for air, but into a recording device operated by engineer Charles Nelson. The machine
etched the sound onto wax discs. Morrison was trying to prove
the value of taping events for archival purposes, not immediate
rebroadcast. When the dirigible exploded, killing many of those
aboard, Morrison kept talking, and the rebroadcast of that recording on NBC made him famous overnight.

Shirer had been invited to go on the ill-fated trip as a guest
of the dirigible company owner's public relations firm, so he
was well aware of the flight and where to go for reaction to the
crash. But sleepy, and perhaps irritated about being called, Shirer
suggested Trask call several other print correspondents. A few
hours later, she rang back and insisted that Shirer do the
broadcast. He relented and wrote out a story. Trask took it to
the Air Ministry page by page to be reviewed by a government
censor. The lines in the script in which Shirer had written that
the Nazis suspected sabotage were ordered deleted.[1]

His voice quavering, Shirer started his first broadcast. "So nervous when I began my broadcast that my voice skipped up and down the scale and my lips and throat grew parched, but after the first page gradually lost my fright. Fear I will never make a broadcaster, but felt relieved I did not have microphone fright, which I understand makes people speechless before a microphone." [2]

While he was well-versed in newspaper journalism, radio was a different story. Shirer had been born in Chicago on February 23, 1904. A graduate of Coe College in Cedar Rapids, he was a true Midwesterner, having lived first in Chicago and then in Cedar Rapids, where he became friends with artist Grant Wood. The move to Iowa came after his forty-one-year-old father, an attorney, died of peritonitis following an appendix operation.

Cedar Rapids had a population of about 35,000 at the beginning of World War I, and two afternoon newspapers. But world news was largely brought to Shirer by the *Chicago Tribune*, which came every morning. At the beginning of his teens, Shirer got into the habit of reading the papers from the front page to the obituary columns. When he was thirteen, he started working after school and on weekends, mostly carting stuff around warehouses. He was a big kid and looked older than his age.

By the time he was sixteen, Shirer was a high school correspondent for one of the Cedar Rapids papers. In the summer, he got a job with a tent crew on the chautauqua circuit, and wound up seeing a good deal of middle America that year and the next. [3]

In college, Shirer worked mornings, weekends, and summers for two years on the *Cedar Rapids Republican*, starting at twenty-five dollars a week. He was also editor of the college weekly, the *Cosmos*. Shirer was on the track team and the debate squad. After graduation, he left for a grand tour of Europe, his mode of transit being a cattle boat. He landed a job with the Paris edition of the *Chicago Tribune* in 1925 and covered other beats for the *Tribune* until 1933, when he switched to the Universal News Service. He had married an Austrian woman in 1931.

So radio was something which Shirer knew about but had not heard much of himself. "I left this country in '25. Radio was just coming in then. I heard some when I was in college, but I went to Europe right after graduation in '25. So I didn't hear much radio. And it was rather behind (America) in Europe, so I didn't hear much in Europe until sometime later."[4]

Since Universal appeared to be going out of business in the summer of 1937, and with his wife pregnant with their first child, Shirer started looking around for another job. On vacation in England in July, he was given a note of introduction to Murrow by a mutual friend. But the two never got together because the Shirers went to the country home of author Paul Gallico, and from there, directly to France. They never got to London again during the trip.

Several weeks later, Universal did go under, and officials of the company which absorbed it, International News Service, decided to release a number of the Universal staff members, including Shirer. The notice of dismissal came on the teletype machine in the Berlin INS bureau. Shirer finished typing the story he was writing and then took a walk to help work off the shock. He did not see, until he returned from his stroll, a second wire—one which had arrived ten minutes before the notice of termination. It had been sent from Murrow,[5] who was in Salzburg arranging a broadcast. The message was brief: "Will you have dinner with me at the Adlon Friday night?" Shirer wired back: "Delighted."[6]

Shirer described their August 20, 1937, meeting in *Berlin Diary*:

As I walked up to him I was a little taken aback by his handsome face. Just what you would expect from radio, I thought. He had asked me for dinner, I considered, to pump me for dope for a radio talk he must make from Berlin. We walked into the bar and there was something in his talk that began disarming me. Something in his eyes that was not Hollywood. . . . He said he had something on his mind. He said he was looking for an experienced foreign correspondent to open a CBS office on the Continent. He could not cover all of Europe from London.[7]

Murrow offered Shirer the job at the same salary he had been making with Universal. But before it became official, Shirer had to pass a voice audition. Everything went wrong when he took it on September 5. Claire Trask, who was to introduce him, had forgotten part of the script and had to run out to get it, returning only a few minutes before air time. The microphone was too high and was stuck in that position. With less than a minute to air, Shirer got up on some packing crates to reach the mike and made his report. A week went by with no word from Murrow. Shirer got a sort of job offer from the *New York Times*, but at a reduced salary. On September 13, Murrow called to say Shirer had been hired and would start October 1, and his office would be in Vienna, "a neutral and central spot" from which Shirer could handle continental arrangements.[8]

The delay in approval was indeed Shirer's announcing abilities. Paley claims that as early as 1930 he and Klauber had decided that reporting would be rated ahead of announcing. But a good amount of attention was being paid to how those who read the news sounded. In 1935, Raymond Swing, while doing a weekly piece at 2:45 P.M. for CBS's "Columbia School of the Air," had gotten Klauber's attention. While judging the content of Swing's commentary on developments overseas to be excellent, Klauber disliked the delivery.[9] He may have found Swing's delivery, as others did, to be excessively suave. Swing tended to give authentic pronunciations to foreign names and places, a practice which seemed to set him apart from most Americans.

Murrow, too, appreciated Swing's broad knowledge, and had asked him to deliver a nightly commentary during the 1936 elections. But Murrow was quickly informed that Klauber had banned Swing from the network. Later that year, Swing moved to Mutual, where he gained a loyal following, especially in the first years of the war. He had a far larger audience in the British Commonwealth. Swing broadcast weekly to the BBC, giving his perspective on events in America. The program had first been suggested by President Roosevelt in 1934 to BBC Chief John Reith, in an effort to improve British understanding of the New Deal. A profile of Swing in *The New Yorker* claimed Swing's voice, however objectionable to some, had become the best known in the world. This was in large part because the BCC often sent

out his commentaries on its shortwave world service as well as
domestically.[10]

Shirer was apparently hired at Murrow's insistence, despite
the poor audition. While happy to have a job, he was not pleased
about having to hire print reporters to broadcast. He felt more
qualified than the young reporters who lacked, in his mind, the
background and language skills to thoroughly cover the escalating situation in Europe. And he did not like scouting out
singing groups for CBS, referring to it as a child's job. "It was
annoying. I didn't quite realize it [would be that way] because
I was out of a job. I took that job because I liked Murrow, and
I had a feeling there was a big future for radio journalism. But
it did annoy me because a lot of times I couldn't get the head
of the wire service and newspaper bureaus to broadcast, usually, and I had to pick people who didn't know as much about
Berlin as I did."[11]

Nevertheless, Murrow and Shirer settled into the task of securing broadcasts for Columbia. The younger network had at
least "traded up," matching their two young representatives
against the veterans from NBC, Bate and Jordan. Murrow and
Bate had become friends, although Bate was old enough to be
Murrow's father. One version of their first meeting shows that
after Saerchinger introduced the two in the lobby at Broadcasting House, Murrow challenged Bate to step outside and settle
the question of network superiority at once. Bate, hoping that
Murrow was displaying a sense of humor, assured him that the
competition between NBC and CBS need not be that stren-
uous.[12]

The situation was different for Shirer. One reason CBS wanted
a representative on the continent was the superiority NBC held
in broadcasting from Germany, Austria, and Hungary. NBC had
signed agreements several years before which gave the network better access to broadcasting facilities in those countries.[13] Shirer had to shoulder most of the burden of convincing
the broadcasting authorities in those countries that NBC was
not the national radio of the United States, and that there should
be equal access for both networks. Murrow also took the same
tack when arranging broadcasts from the continent. In Britain,

however, all foreign representatives were treated equally, and their needs taken care of in an efficient manner.

CBS, NBC, and Mutual were reaping the benefits of the growing popularity of radio in America. By 1938, it had become America's favorite leisure activity, according to a survey conducted for *Fortune*. Radio was favored by 18.8 percent of those polled, compared to 17.3 percent who preferred movies. The favorite programs? Jack Benny, Major Bowes, and news. And the favorite personalities were led by Benny, but then followed by Boake Carter and Lowell Thomas, with Edwin C. Hill also in the top ten. And in the northeastern part of the country, Thomas was first, Carter second, and Benny third.[14]

In the first weeks of 1938, the biggest news for Shirer was the impending birth of his child. A baby girl was born on February 26, 1938, while Shirer was out of town arranging a broadcast. As the situation in Austria disintegrated, Shirer was disappointed not to be telling Americans about it. He wrote on March 4: "I feel a little empty, being here on the scene but doing no actual reporting. Curious radio doesn't want a firsthand report. But New York hasn't asked for anything, being chiefly concerned with educational broadcasts. I must do . . . in a few days a school children's chorus or something."[15]

While Shirer was in Ljubljana, Yugoslavia, overseeing that program for the Columbia School of the Air, the final events leading to the *Anschluss* began to occur. Murrow was in Warsaw, Poland, where he had been supervising another segment for the same network program. Trying to resist the pressure being applied by Hitler, Austrian Chancellor Kurt von Schuschnigg had called for a plebiscite on the question of Austrian independence. It had been scheduled for Sunday, March 13.

The news of the election was passed to Shirer when he arrived in Vienna on Friday morning, March 11. The taxi driver told him, and then his housekeeper handed him enough newspapers to bring him up to date while he ate his breakfast. In midafternoon, Shirer went to visit his wife, who was still in the hospital following a difficult delivery. When he emerged, it was being announced that the election was off. By dark, the Nazis were in control, and all that was left for Chancellor von

Schuschnigg to reveal on the state radio station was that the end had come for an independent Austria.

The first news of the *Anschluss* came to American radio listeners on Friday morning, and the source was the wire services. CBS had the Associated Press, United Press, International News Service, and Transradio in addition to Press-Radio Bureau, but information was sketchy. And no word had come from CBS's European representatives. Shirer had tried to reach Murrow shortly after 6 P.M., but he was not in his Warsaw hotel room. Shirer then tried to arrange a broadcast using Austrian national radio facilities, but found Nazis in control, and they were not allowing any outside broadcasts. Paley had the same experience from long distance when he tried to determine what was going on. He had been home that day with a fever caused by a cold. Klauber phoned him with word of the refusal to allow Shirer to report. And not realizing the Nazis were in total control, Paley resolved to talk by phone directly with Erich von Kunsti, head of the Austrian broadcast agency RVG. "I told him how distressing it was that his organization was not allowing us the use of the facilities we needed to broadcast from there. In a tearful voice he broke in to say, 'I am sorry, Mr. Paley, I am no longer in charge here. I cannot do anything. . . . I would if I could.' There was a sob and then a click. The connection was broken and he was gone."[16]

After alternating between trying unsuccessfully to reach Murrow and trying unsuccessfully to convince the Nazis to let him broadcast, Shirer went home at 3 A.M. on March 12. Shortly after he got there, Murrow phoned. The opening lines were brief:

Shirer: The enemy has crossed the goal line.
Murrow: Are you sure?
Shirer: I'm paid to be sure.[17]

The two men talked over the possibilities for broadcasting. Murrow had already talked to White, who was still relying on the wires, about the options. Shirer pointed out that Nazi control of Austria meant Nazi censorship of broadcasts, even if RVG facilities became available to CBS. Murrow suggested that Shirer fly to London to be assured of an uncensored report. Murrow would go to Vienna.

With only an hour of sleep, Shirer went to the airport, which already sported a number of German war planes. The gestapo was in control. "At first they said no planes would be allowed to take off. Then they cleared the London plane. But I could not get on. I offered fantastic sums to several passengers for their places. Most of them were Jews and I could not blame them for turning me down. Next was the plane to Berlin. I got on that."[18]

In Berlin, Shirer caught a Dutch plane to London and wrote his broadcast script while in the air. From the BBC, he told his story to listeners in America at 11:30 P.M. English time, about dinner time in the East.

Austria's resistance to Nazi Socialism actually collapsed at 6:15 P.M. yesterday when it was announced on the radio that the plebiscite had been indefinitely postponed. . . . When the radio announcement came over the loudspeaker, the Fatherland Front people and the workers melted away and stole home as best they could. On the other hand, it was the signal for the Nazis to come out and capture the streets of the capital. . . . I saw a strange sight: twenty men, bent down, formed a human pyramid, and a little man—I suppose he was picked for his weight—scampered over a lot of shoulders and, clutching a huge swastika flag, climbed to the balcony of the Chancellery.[19]

Murrow had difficulty with his plane connections as well. He got from Warsaw to Berlin, but could not get into Vienna. So he chartered a twenty-seven-seat Lufthansa passenger plane for $1,000 and, in solitary luxury, flew to Vienna.

The fact that Jordan was based in Basel may have contributed to NBC being beaten on initial coverage of the *Anschluss*. After hearing Schuschnigg's call for a plebiscite Wednesday night on the radio, Jordan had taken a Thursday morning train toward Vienna. There were several delays, but when it stopped in Innsbruck, Jordan noticed the Austrian policemen on the train were wearing Nazi arm bands. Instead of getting off and asking what had happened, Jordan just asked the conductor, who said he did not know. "When we started moving again, I decided to go back to bed. There was nothing I could do but wait until we reached Vienna."[20]

Jordan did not arrive until late Friday. He also tried to broadcast from the RVG studios, but found that Kunsti, who had assisted NBC many times on past broadcasts, had been replaced by his assistant, "a neophyte Nazi."[21] Kunsti had been confined to his office, and was down to his last cigarette. With no way to get his story out, Jordan went out and returned with the requested American cigarettes for his friend. Kunsti was soon released, and remained with the RVG as an accountant.

NBC's long relationship with the Austrian broadcasting agency paid dividends when Jordan made the first broadcast to America from occupied Austria on Saturday, March 12. The report was censored in theory, but perhaps not in practice. Jordan claims in *Beyond All Fronts*: "Fortunately, rules and regulations were then still being applied with a good deal of common sense, that same common sense George N. Schuster had in mind when he once pointed out that the difference between German and French policemen is that the latter know when not to enforce the rules! So by the time I succeeded in calling New York to ask for a 'period' I was all set to go on the air with the first eyewitness account of Hitler's march on Vienna, straight from the scene and uncensored."[22]

Jordan had been broadcasting for about ten minutes when an alert engineer signaled him to pick up a headset which was plugged into the Austrian radio program. While still talking live to America, Jordan put the ear piece on and heard the bulletin that Hitler had arrived in Linz. Jordan had been to that city a number of times, and he filled a few minutes of air time with a description of the city on the Danube in upper Austria. The engineer, on cue from Jordan, would cut in the RVG program and relay it to NBC. "Presently I heard a voice and tried to identify it. 'Some local orator is now addressing the crowd of 300,000 people[23] on the Linz City Hall Square. Let me find out who it is. . . . Oh, it's Hitler himself!' And within a split second we turned over and broadcast the 'Fuehrer's' 300-word speech which sealed the fate of Austria by incorporating her into the Reich."[24]

Jordan delivered the historic event to NBC listeners while it was happening. His broadcast was heard before Shirer did his from London, the difference being the ethical compromises, if any, under which Jordan's was made. Shirer feels his London broadcast, and others he and Murrow made over the next few days, were an important step toward establishing broadcast foreign correspondence. "We took advantage of an event which allowed us to do it (instead of hire print men) and that was the *Anschluss*. As I recall, we didn't even ask them, we just went on the air and they were glad to have us. And that changed the whole thing. It was just one of those accidents that happened. If it hadn't been a big event like that, the networks were too stupid to change their policy, I think."[25]

Whether the networks would have changed is moot. The events in Europe would continue to demand coverage by reporters with first allegiance to the networks, who could speak for themselves to America. A more immediate change was inauguration of the European Roundup, which was a key factor in the revolution of broadcast news coverage.

NOTES

1. Print dispatches to America were not censored at that time, and Shirer was surprised to find that his broadcast was to be reviewed.

2. William L. Shirer, *Berlin Diary* (New York: Knopf, 1941), p. 73.

3. William L. Shirer, *Twentieth Century Journey—a Memoir of a Life and the Times. The Start: 1904–1930* (New York: Simon & Schuster, 1976), p. 163. Shirer, like Murrow, lied about his age in applying for the job.

4. William L. Shirer, interview with the author, October 11, 1980.

5. Saerchinger had been known as CBS European representative. Paley and others refer to Murrow as European Director when he first went overseas for the network. Perhaps this apparent title change reflected a structural change at the network.

6. Shirer, *Berlin Diary*, p. 79.

7. Ibid., pp. 80–81.

8. Ibid., pp. 82–83.

9. Culbert, *News for Everyman*, p. 102.

10. *The New Yorker*, November 21, 1942, p. 28.

11. Shirer, interview with the author, October 11, 1980.

12. Kendrick, *Prime Time*, p. 145.

13. For examples of the ramifications of the agreements, see Shirer,

Berlin Diary, p. 145; Jordan, *Beyond All Fronts*, p. 184; and Kendrick, *Prime Time*, p. 146.

14. *Fortune*, Vol. 17, No. 1, January 1938.

15. Shirer, *Berlin Diary*, p. 94.

16. Paley, *As It Happened*, p. 130.

17. Quoted in M. L. Stein, *Under Fire: The Story of American War Correspondents* (New York: Messner, 1968), p. 235.

18. Shirer, *Berlin Diary*, p. 102.

19. Quoted in Paley, *As It Happened*, p. 132.

20. Jordan, *Beyond All Fronts*, p. 189.

21. Ibid., p. 192.

22. Ibid., p. 193.

23. Jordan was apparently willing to pass along without qualification the RVG announcer's estimate.

24. Jordan, *Beyond All Fronts*, pp. 193–94.

25. Shirer, interview with the author, October 11, 1980.

3 · The European Roundup

CBS had failed to get a broadcast out of Vienna in the first few hours after the Nazi takeover. But as he nursed his cold at home in America, Paley thought about what the *Anschluss* meant, and wondered what was being said about it in London, Paris, Rome, and other European capitals. Was there a way to link those cities in a broadcast? There had been any number of previous broadcasts with multilocation links, including NBC's tenth anniversary broadcast. CBS had done two programs recently which featured European leaders speaking from their capitals, but they had taken months to arrange. Paley wanted to move quickly. "I called Klauber and asked him to put it up to the engineers. Their first reaction was gloomy—it couldn't be done. I insisted that there must be some way. Within an hour, Klauber called back to say that it would be a very tricky operation, but it probably could be worked out. I urged him to proceed with haste."[1]

Like many news decisions at CBS, Paley and Klauber did the deciding and White carried it out. With technical elements to ascertain, and his only two men in Europe in the air, the broadcast was not scheduled until after Shirer was in London on Sunday afternoon. Shirer quotes White as saying: "We want a European roundup tonight. One A.M. your time. We want you and some member of Parliament from London, Ed Murrow of course from Vienna, and American newspaper correspondents from Berlin, Paris, and Rome. A half-hour show, and I'll telephone you the exact time for each capital in about an hour. Can you and Murrow do it?"[2]

Shirer answered yes, but he did not know how to make all

the arrangements, especially since air time was less than eight hours away.[3]

I put in a long-distance call to Murrow in Vienna. And as valuable minutes ticked away I considered what to do. The more I thought about it, the simpler it became. Murrow and I have newspaper friends, American correspondents, in every capital in Europe. We also know personally the directors and chief engineers of the various European broadcasting systems whose technical facilities we must use. I called Edgar Mowrer in Paris, Frank Gervasi in Rome, Pierre Huss in Berlin, and the directors and chief engineers of PTT in Paris, EIAR in Turin, and the RRG in Berlin.[4]

When Murrow returned Shirer's call, he offered advice on technical arrangements and took responsibility for Berlin and Vienna. The line from Vienna to Berlin had been opened the day before when Jordan broadcast for NBC, but the German military was using it and it might not be available. And both the Vienna and the Berlin reports would have to pass through Nazi censorship. That left Shirer with London, Rome, and Paris.

There were more problems. Paris has no strong shortwave transmitter. Rome did, but the proper officials needed for authorization could not be reached; it was Sunday. Mowrer, Paris correspondent for the *Chicago Daily News*, agreed to end his weekend in the country early and go back to Paris. Special lines would have to be arranged to get a signal from him to a transmitter that was powerful enough. Huss and Gervasi, both INS correspondents, needed permission from their New York headquarters. It was obtained. Then Gervasi called from Rome. The Italians could not arrange the broadcast on such short notice. So Shirer had Gervasi's dispatch taken down in shorthand over the phone, and he read it from London. With two hours to air, Shirer convinced Labour M.P. Ellen Wilkinson to also end her weekend in the country and drive to the BBC studios in London.

Gervasi's report was still being taken by a stenographer as Shirer went over the last-minute times and cues with producers in New York. White had arranged for Democratic Senator

Lewis B. Schwellenbach from the state of Washington to com-
ment from Washington, D.C. Confident that his broadcast would
come off, White had also started putting promotional announcements on the network even before he had called Shirer.

At 1 A.M. Monday, March 14, 1938, in London, and 8 P.M.
on March 13 in New York, the "European Roundup" began.
Robert Trout was introduced as "The Voice of CBS News," and
told the audience:

The program "St. Louis Blues" will not be heard tonight. . . . The
world's spotlight, for three days fastened upon Austria, is shared tonight by London's Ten Downing Street; by the Quai D'Orsay, whose
buildings of state line the Seine River in Paris, and by other chancel-
leries throughout the world. To bring you the picture of Europe tonight Columbia now presents a special broadcast which will include
pick ups direct from London, from Paris, and such other European
capitals as have communication channels available. . . . Columbia be-
gins its radio tour of Europe's capital cities with a trans-oceanic pickup
from London.[5]

Not a cue was missed. A half-hour after it started, the first
European Roundup ended precisely on time. Talking via the
shortwave link after the broadcast was over, White pro-
nounced the roundup a success and told reporters he wanted
a second one the next day. H. V. Kaltenborn, who was in the
CBS New York studios during the inaugural broadcast, was impressed by what he heard. "The technical set up to tie up and
untie the entire network in a matter of seconds or to bring together New York and five European capitals for a round-robin
discussion involved the most ingenious devices, some of them
developed on the spot by inventive engineers who looked to
meet a new challenge."[6]

The first roundup, which later evolved into the World News
Roundup, still a feature of the CBS radio network, should be
understood in the context of the impact the news had on
America. Robert Bendiner, as managing editor of *The Nation*,
followed developments closely. "Piecemeal, by radio and dispatch, the story of Vienna's ordeal reached us. . . . Weekend
news cables carry the story of how Schuschnigg, in the very

room where his predecessor Dollfuss had been shot to death by Nazi assassins, takes to the microphone. . . . It was hard to realize what we were hearing and reading was the death of an ancient state, the opening of a cultivated city to a barbarian. For the moment we were caught up in the immediate drama and the sensationalism of the news."[7]

The second European Roundup followed the same pattern as the first. Once again, Gervasi could not arrange a broadcast from Rome, and his report was phoned to London, where Shirer read it. The supporting cast was different, except for Gervasi, with Phillip Jordan, Kenneth Downs, Albion Ross, and Senator Ryan Duffy speaking. It was heard Monday night in America.[8]

Murrow had been heard in a solo broadcast earlier that day, and as the annexation was formalized, he and Shirer continued to report. They also lined up agency and newspaper reporters to augment the CBS coverage. On Tuesday, March 16, Murrow arranged for at least three broadcasts. First, Hitler spoke from the Heldenplatz before a crowd of 100,000. The speech was heard at 5 A.M. in New York. CBS listeners on the East Coast heard Murrow summarize it two hours later, and that afternoon Murrow reported again, this time discussing how quickly Austria seemed to become a Nazi country. Hitler left Vienna that night and went back to Munich. In London, Shirer arranged for Winston Churchill to broadcast a talk. Churchill wanted $500 to do it.

By Wednesday, things had quieted down to the extent that Murrow and Shirer agreed on the telephone to trade places again. Murrow, however, would wait for Shirer in Vienna before departing for London. Shirer wrote in his diary: "The crisis is over. I think we've found something, though, for radio, in these roundups."[9] In the weeks to follow, and through the summer, there were no regularly scheduled roundups. But Murrow and Shirer did broadcast frequently. In the second week of April, Shirer's wife and baby were finally able to leave the hospital. He tenderly carried them up the stairs to their apartment. And a few days later, he confidently wrote: "I think radio talks by Ed and me are now established. Birth of the 'radio foreign correspondent,' so to speak."[10]

Another crisis, however, this one in September 1938, would

be needed to firmly establish the new species. From September 11 through the end of the month, NBC and CBS provided nearly around-the-clock coverage of the Munich Crisis. Until then, neither network had made a significant move to upgrade their European staffs. Bate and Jordan continued to represent NBC, and Murrow and Shirer were on board for CBS. But the two CBS men did take advantage of the lull that summer to meet several times and discuss the future of radio coverage from Europe. Both agreed that war was coming, and that better equipment was needed for broadcasting to America. They also felt CBS needed to build up its staff because the papers and wire services would have first call on their reporters when developments escalated.

Still, the bulk of their assignments involved entertainment programming, and when a newsman was needed, the networks preferred that Shirer and Murrow hire a stringer. At one point, Shirer guessed that he had been wrong about the birth of the radio foreign correspondent.

There had been an increase in the number of commentators on American radio, though. Dorothy Thompson was heard on NBC Red, and General Hugh S. Johnson on Blue. Raymond Gram Swing had greatly increased his following on Mutual, but still found himself unsponsored. Kaltenborn's broadcasts on CBS were also without sponsorship but were very popular. And Lowell Thomas did have commercial backing on his less-topical NBC reports.[11]

As the Czechoslovakian situation began to escalate, Shirer prepared to go to Prague and cover events there. One further indication of the attitude at CBS toward correspondents is contained in an article Shirer wrote for *Atlantic Monthly* after the war in Europe was underway.

I hopped a plane for Prague. But before leaving my headquarters in Geneva, Switzerland, I cabled the New York office of the Columbia Broadcasting System, suggesting that I give a daily five-minute talk from the Czech capital. My home office thought I was crazy. Perhaps five minutes once a week on Sunday afternoons—but every day! Within the week, however, we were broadcasting daily not only from Prague, but also from London and Paris and Rome and Berlin and Godesberg and Munich.[12]

Shirer arrived in Czechoslovakia on September 10, 1938, in time to arrange a talk by President Eduard Beneš. The network also carried a report that day from Nuremberg, where Herman Göring told a Nazi Party rally: "A petty segment of Europe is harassing human beings. . . . This miserable pygmy race (the Czechs) without culture—no one knows where it came from— is oppressing a cultured people and behind it is Moscow and the eternal mask of the Jew devil."[13]

Perhaps what they heard from Göring convinced CBS officials that more coverage was needed from Shirer, because he received approval for the five-minute programs from Prague the next day. There was one condition: Shirer was to cable cancellation to New York if there were no new developments on a particular day.

But starting the very next day, there were enough developments to cause CBS to carry Shirer's reports not once a day, but five and six times a day. On September 12, 1938, Hitler made a speech in Nuremberg, which was carried in America. It contained a demand for self-determination for the people of Sudetenland. The Munich Crisis had begun.

Central to the crisis were three meetings between Hitler and Neville Chamberlain, the first in Berchtesgaden, the second in Godesberg, and the last in Munich.

CBS carried 15l shortwave broadcasts during that period, NBC, 147. Murrow made thirty-five himself from London. Bate too stayed mostly in London. The bulk of the reporting came from Jordan and Shirer.

For the first four nights of the crisis, Shirer's reports from Prague did not get through, probably due to atmospheric conditions, and he was forced to cable them to New York. After that, though, he became the mainstay of CBS coverage, although personally frustrated by his inability to read the Czechoslovakian papers, printed in one of the few European languages he did not speak.

As events shifted to Godesberg, Shirer made one of the more unusual broadcasts in the history of radio. On September 20, 1938, he had been scheduled to do a report at 10:30 P.M. But that was also when his train to Godesberg was scheduled to depart. Instead of approving cancellation of the broadcast, White prodded Shirer into doing it from the train platform. White moved up the air time a half-hour, and engineers from the German radio agency set up a microphone. Shirer made a lengthy broadcast, interviewing a half-dozen correspondents who were also taking the train. The German trains were prompt, and Shirer noticed toward the end of his report that his train was starting to move out of the station. With a sentence-long conclusion, he ended his report and ran for the train, which he caught.

Jordan scored two impressive beats during the crisis, the first one at Godesberg. Because he knew the proprietor of the hotel where Hitler was staying and where most of the meetings were taking place, Jordan was able to set up a microphone in the pantry. This allowed him to peek through a window into the main lobby and watch the European leaders as they came and went from the conference room.

Greater advantage was gained at Munich, where Jordan once again got closer to the principals than other American reporters and put his proximity to good use. The foreign radio men were required to use a German radio studio about twenty blocks from the Brown House where representatives of the four powers were meeting. The German broadcasters themselves were set up in the attic of the Brown House, a fact which Jordan discovered through judicious questioning during a routine tour of the building for American print and broadcast correspondents proir to the start of the sessions.

Taking the attitude that ''there are no obstacles in this world which cannot be conquered, if conquered they must be,''[14] Jordan resolved to gain access to the German equipment. He got his chance that night when he walked behind Schmidt Hansen, a German radio employee, as Hansen showed his credentials at a checkpoint outside the building. The two men then went in the back door of the building and up to the radio room. Once inside the house and on his own, Jordan found his way to the main lobby and then went back to the attic, where an alarmed Hansen tried to get Jordan to go back to the facilities were the rest of the foreign radio people were. But Jordan got on a phone to Hansen's superior in Berlin and managed to get permission to use the German radio link to pass a message to NBC in New York. Then he went down to the lobby so he could keep an eye on the conference room.

About one o'clock in the morning I noticed a group of Italian officers leaving the conference room. As they walked by I heard them drop a remark which seemed to indicate that the meeting was about to come to a close. "Andiamoncene!" said one of the men. "Let's pack our grips." That was my cue. I dashed upstairs and called New York once more.

"Stand by, NBC! Important announcement expected momentarily! Stand by!"

Back in the lobby, I could see that the meeting was actually nearing its end. I noticed Sir William Strang of the British delegation, leaning against a railing of the big marble staircase. To him I was able to explain the importance of our securing the official English text of whatever communique was going to be issued. He promised to do his best.[15]

Jordan nearly missed his scoop, however, because he ran back upstairs to the radio room to issue another advisory to New York. When he ran back downstairs, the meeting had broken up, and Jordan had to chase the British delegation, shouting for attention. Sir William Strang and Sir Horace Wilson stopped, and after a moment's whispered conversation, a copy of the official communique was given to Jordan. He had obtained the terms of the agreement so quickly that when he appeared upstairs the Germans did not believe he had the real McCoy and were not going to let him broadcast. A sharp argument followed for a few minutes, but finally Jordan did get his news out.[16]

Shirer was appalled at being beaten by Jordan, but his estimation of how much Jordan's relationship with the German radio agency had to do with the scoop seems to be mistaken. "Because of his company's special position in Germany, he was allowed exclusive use of Hitler's radio studio in the Fuehrerhaus, where the conference has been taking place. . . . Unable to use this studio on the spot, I stayed close to the only other outlet, the studio of the Munich station, and arranged with several English and American friends to get me the document. . . . Demaree Bess was first to arrive with a copy, but, alas, we were late."[17]

Murrow had been able to tell CBS listeners about the agreement by picking up a German broadcast while giving a report of his own from London, but Jordan was clearly the winner in that internetwork battle. NBC added to its triumph by obtaining an exclusive interview with Chamberlain when he returned to England.

While the Munich meeting of the four powers was being held, a huge storm was battering the Atlantic coastline, particularly the New England states. It struck with little warning on September 21, and, before subsiding, killed nearly 700 people. Using the advancements forged in reporting from Europe, the networks covered those events as well in their around-the-clock coverage.

In America, a 59-year-old man put on a display of physical stamina which outstripped the efforts of the younger foreign correspondents. H. V. Kaltenborn provided the continuity for the reports coming in from overseas, doing 102 separate broadcasts over the three weeks. Some were just bulletins, as short as a minute or two. Others lasted up to two hours, with Kaltenborn sometimes simultaneously translating speeches in French or German.

During the crisis there were fourteen roundups like the ones during the Vienna coverage in the spring. CBS had 115 affiliates at the time, and with the push of one button, the network could be heard on all of them if news developments merited interrupting scheduled programming.

That button was in Studio Nine on the seventeenth floor, the studio that was to become the main broadcast news studio for the CBS radio network until operations were moved across town to Fifty-seventh Street, a quarter of a century later. It had been completed in the days just before the Munich Crisis began and was Paul White's baby. According to a CBS release, White had put in hours equal to Kaltenborn's during the crisis. "Not even the grueling job of maintaining a twenty-four-hour vigil over a crisis can for a minute destroy his sense of humor—a safety valve giving automatic service whenever the seemingly endless strain nears the breaking point. It's also the newsman in Paul White which refuses to go home, even to change a necktie—for fear the BIG story in the crisis might break the minute he takes his eyes away from the teletype machine's cables."[18] Paley was also closely monitoring the work of the CBS newsroom, which had about sixty employees then. "I was either at the studio or constantly listening from wherever I might be. Live news and on-the-spot broadcasting made their mark. I was so excited that I sent Murrow and Shirer this cable: 'Columbia's coverage of the European crisis is superior to its competitors and is probably the best job of its kind ever done in radio broadcasting.' "[19]

Some idea of how CBS was able to augment its two representatives is indicated in *Crisis*, a booklet CBS published after the Munich events were over. It was not intended for the general public but rather was a public relations tool aimed particularly at sponsors. Among those who reported for CBS were:

Melvin Whiteleather, Associated Press
John Whittaker, *Chicago Daily News* Syndicate
Vernon Bartlett, *London News Chronicle* Diplomatic Corresondent
Phillip Jordan, *London News Chronicle*
Matthew Houghton, *Toronto Star*
Kenneth Downs, International News Service, Paris Bureau Chief
Maurice Hindus, International News Service, Prague
Pierre Huss, International News Service, Berlin
Selkirk Panton, *London Daily Express*
Ralph Barnes, *New York Herald-Tribune*, Berlin
Webb Miller, Associated Press
Frank Gervasi, United Press, Rome Bureau Chief
Thomas Grandin, United Press[20]

Kaltenborn appraised the reaction Americans had to the nearly continuous coverage: "The intensity with which America listened to the radio reports of the Munich crisis was without parallel in radio history. Portable radio sets which had just been developed had a tremendous sale."[21]

Writing about the period between the wars, Jonathan Daniels evaluated the September network coverage: "All this was not news of America but it was startling American news. Even the possibility of war was, of course, far off, as isolationists and many more agreed. Still, there was a sort of buzz of planes in the ears of even safe Americans. More and more the jitters was a transatlantic contagion not easily quarantined."[22]

A more formal measure of the impact of the Munich broadcasts came from an American Institute of Public Opinion poll. It revealed that seven of every ten polled preferred radio as their news source during the events of September.[23] In a matter of weeks, radio had over taken the newspapers. The live coverage had made extra editions a less profitable venture. Within six months, the Press-Radio Bureau would be dissolved, and the Associated Press members would begin taking the steps which would lead to providing AP news to broadcasters. The local stations increased their news commitments, one indication being that by 1939, 293 radio stations had subscribed to the United Press, 141 had INS, and 177 Transradio.

Those who conclude, though, that radio contributed greatly to the decline of newspaper readership should reconsider. A study completed in 1940 by several top media researchers found that radio war coverage actually increased newspaper patronage. Hadley Cantril and his associates concluded that while news listening did increase sharply during a crisis such as Munich, "The greater the interest in news, the greater is the preference for the newspaper over radio news. Generally, as interest in events increases, the listener's desire to know more sends him to other outlets, principally the newspaper. Specifically, those surveyed for the study who were good readers found reading to be a more efficient process of informing themselves. Those who were non-readers became less satisfied with radio and developed into newspaper readers."[24]

This pattern could not apply when events moved so swiftly that the only way to follow them was on radio. Despite the advances made in the name of broadcast news, it was a relatively small part of the network prime-time programming during the winter of 1938–39. Programs counted as "Commercial Evening Network Time Devoted to 'Commentators, News and Talks' " were 6.7 percent of total programming. Two years later, the figure nearly doubled, and by the end of the war, it nearly tripled.[25]

Writing a year after the Munich Crisis, Kaltenborn pointed

out the challenge the networks were facing; there is a difference between covering a brief crisis and a war. "What can be
done during a three-week crisis cannot be continued for months.
Neither listeners nor broadcasters could stand the strain. Obviously, the broadcasters have now had to settle down to a basis of operations that will meet the test of a long drawn out
conflict."[26]

Eight days after the crisis ended, Murrow and Shirer met in
Paris to talk about the future. They thought Munich had only
further ensured war would come, and that it would start after
the next harvest. They also pinpointed Poland as the site of the
next crisis, and resolved to help the Poles improve their shortwave facilities. And once again they decided the CBS staff in
Europe needed to be augmented with American newspeople.

Mutual, which had carried reports from Europe during the
crisis, but not nearly as many as NBC or CBS, did not yet have
a full-time representative in Europe. NBC stuck with Bate and
Jordan. And while war would come after the next harvest, it
took almost a year until a new transmitter was built in Poland
and a third staff member was added for CBS.

One other event in 1938 revealed just how much impact the
network coverage in September had on Americans. Exactly one
month after the papers had been signed at Munich, a radio
drama which imitated the kind of live coverage heard in September on the networks scared many of the people who heard
it. The *Mercury Theatre on the Air* presentation of "The War of
the Worlds" caused more than a million people to believe New
Jersey had been invaded by Martians. The broadcast was directed by Orson Welles, and the script was written by Howard
Koch with supervision by John Houseman. As they worked on
the many changes made in transferring H. G. Wells's story to
an East Coast setting, what Houseman and Koch had been
hearing on the radio became a part of their drama.

After a short introduction which made it clear that a radio
play was being presented, the broadcast became a simulated
radio program, starting with a weather forecast and then
switching to a remote broadcast of dance music from a New York
hotel. Within a few seconds, the music was faded so an announcer could say:

Ladies and gentlemen, we interrupt our program of dance music to bring you a special bulletin from the Intercontinental Radio News. At twenty minutes before eight, Central Time, Professor Farrell of the Mount Jennings Observatory, Chicago, Illinois, reports observing several explosions of incandescent gas, occurring at regular intervals on the planet Mars. The spectroscope indicates the gas to be hydrogen and moving toward the earth with enormous velocity. Professor Pierson of the observatory at Princeton confirms Farrell's observation, and describes the phenomenon as "like a jet of blue flame shot from a gun."
We return you to the music of Ramon Raquello.[27]

The music was heard for just a couple of beats and then there was a second interruption with more details, and a switch to Princeton. "Carl Phillips, our commentator,"[28] interviewed a professor of astronomy about the explosions and the dance music was never heard again. Instead, the "live" coverage went on to include more eyewitness reports, more switches, a telephone report, and even bulletins from the "Intercontinental Radio News."

Those who tuned in late, perhaps switching over from the more popular Edgar Bergen-Charlie McCarthy program, or people who had not been listening very carefully,[29] were shocked at what they heard. Some reacted with panic, and there were dozens of instances of bizarre and dangerous behavior. An Indianapolis woman is reported to have run into a church screaming "New York is destroyed; it's the end of the world. You might as well go home to die. It's the end of the world."[30]

Listening today to a recording of the broadcast, it may be hard to believe so many people were taken in. The news bulletins seem to come too quickly,[31] the commentator gets to Princeton too soon after the initial report of the explosions, and even Martians take a little while to travel through outer space. But the people who heard it live in 1938 had only recently become familiar with remote news broadcasts. They believed what they heard on the radio. It was night, and people might have been reluctant to go outdoors and seek confirmation or denial of the news. In short, many who heard the broadcast were not sophisticated listeners, although two who did go outside were Princeton geology professors who wanted to locate the crater created when the Martians landed.

On April Fool's Eve, 1940, America's favorite radio enter-
tainer, Jack Benny, held an imaginary phone conversation with
Welles. In it, Benny blamed Welles for a recent series of sunspot storms in North America, and generally tweaked the director's nose for the uproar his program had caused a year and
a half earlier.

A more serious examination of the effect of the *Mercury The-*
atre broadcast was published that year. Edited by Hadley Cantril of Princeton's Radio Research Project, *The Invasion of Mars*
documented the tremendous impact of "The War of the Worlds."
Six million Americans heard the program. And 1.7 million believed it was news, with 1.2 million of those believers frightened by what they heard.

The researchers, funded by a Rockefeller General Education
Board grant of $5,000, concluded that the believers lacked the
ability to perceive the broadcast was just a play. "Critical ability
was affected by other factors tending to create susceptibility.
Most significant of these were universal insecurity, worries,
phobias, fatalism, war fear."[32]

The *New York Times* editors did not need a study to know that
a lot of people had been needlessly frightened. A day after the
broadcast, the paper editorialized about the responsibility of the
networks, blasting CBS for putting something on the air which
caused so much anguish. And the four-year-old Federal Communications Commission responded as well, moving to ban all
dramatized news from the air.

By the end of 1938, NBC had a set of guidelines which its
newsmen were supposed to follow in their broadcasts. The list
resulted from public reaction to "The War of the Worlds," a
Walter Winchell newscast which stated that nine Cornell students had died in a dorm fire without giving further details,
and several other similar incidents. Among the rules:

Early in the evening children are listening in, so sex, crime and juicy
    stories are out. At 11, however, we can be more liberal with our
    treatment and types of news stories.
No suicides.
Be careful about using smiles on the air.
No flash stories about plane crashes, school fires, riots, etc., until
    complete details are available and rescuers have the situation
    under control.[33]

CBS had caught listeners off guard a few years earlier, when an announcer read: "William N. Doak, Secretary of Labor in the Cabinet of President Hoover, died today in Washington." Too many of the listeners picked up only the last part, and thought the former President had died.

Incidents like these sparked both networks to adopt a more conversational broadcast style in newscasts. NBC was depicted as trying "to make their broadcasts sound as though a man has just come home, bursting to tell his family about the collision of two fire trucks he has just seen down the street—conversational, chatty, folksy."[34]

NOTES

1. Paley, *As It Happened*, p. 131.

2. Shirer, *Berlin Diary*, p. 104.

3. Webb Miller had scored a forty-nine-minute beat for the AP in the Italian invasion of Ethiopia. He believed in the theory of Edward Keen that "it was not enough for the correspondent to gather and write the news; the correspondent must know his lines of communication thoroughly and be responsible for the delivery of the story to his home office." The radio men would learn the wisdom of that idea. Webb Miller, *I Found No Peace* (New York: Simon & Schuster, 1936), p. 240.

4. Shirer, *Berlin Diary*, p. 105.

5. The excerpt is taken from a CBS promotional booklet, *Vienna*, published in March 1938.

6. H. V. Kaltenborn, *Fifty Fabulous Years, 1900–1950: A Personal Review* (New York: Putnam, 1950), p. 208.

7. Robert Bendiner, *Just Around the Corner—a Highly Selective History of the 30's* (New York: Harper and Row, 1967), p. 202.

8. In 1958 there was a great deal of media attention on the twentieth anniversary of the first roundup. There was also a luncheon attended by a handful of CBS executives, including Paley, Murrow, Frank Stanton, and Arthur Hayes. Jules Dundes, who by then was a radio network vice-president, remembers with dismay what occurred: "Hayes, as the president of CBS Radio, had tried to publicize the anniversary, although there was no publicity of the luncheon itself. Murrow and Paley threw names at each other. I was appalled at the name dropping that went on. Two men like this? They tried to outdo each other at dropping names." (Interview with the author, July 25, 1980.)

Missing from the dinner as well were White, who had died a few years before in San Diego, and William L. Shirer, who was concentrating on writing books. Both men had been fired by Murrow during his short tenure as CBS news director after the war.

   9. Shirer, *Berlin Diary*, p. 108.

   10. Ibid., p. 112.

   11. Culbert, *News for Everyman*, pp. 16–19.

   12. William L. Shirer, "Berlin Speaking," *Atlantic Monthly*, Vol. 166, No. 3, September 1940, pp. 308–12.

   13. Shirer, *Berlin Diary*, p. 126.

   14. Jordan, *Beyond All Fronts*, p. 218.

   15. Ibid., p. 221.

   16. Ibid., pp. 220–22.

   17. Shirer, *Berlin Diary*, pp. 145–46.

   18. CBS Research Library, New York. CBS biographical service release, dated 9/1/39.

   19. Paley, *As It Happened*, p. 135.

   20. Columbia Broadcasting System, *Crisis*, eds. Jules Dundes and Victor Ratner (New York, 1938), no page number.

   21. Kaltenborn, *Fifty Fabulous Years*, p. 208.

   22. Jonathan Daniels, *The Time Between the Wars—from the Jazz Age and the Depression to Pearl Harbor* (Garden City, N.Y.: Doubleday, 1966), p. 301.

   23. Culbert, *News for Everyman*, p. 74.

   24. Edwin Muller, "Radio and Reading, "*The New Republic*, Vol. 102, No. 8, February 19, 1940, pp. 236–37.

   25. David Dary, *Radio News Handbook* (Thurmont, Md.: TAB Books, 1967), p. 23.

   26. H. V. Kaltenborn, "Covering the Crisis," *Current History*, Vol. 51, No. 2, October 1939, p. 35.

   27. "The War of the Worlds," *Mercury Theater on the Air*, heard on CBS, October 30, 1938.

   28. The actor portraying the reporter had studied the Hindenburg broadcast in preparing for his part.

   29. Four times during the performance it was identified as a play.

   30. Frederick Lewis Allen, *Since Yesterday: The Nineteen-Thirties in America* (New York: Bantam, 1965), p. 262.

   31. There was, however, a joke at CBS during the Munich crisis about "bulletins being interrupted by bulletins."

   32. Hadley Cantril, *The Invasion from Mars* (New York: Harper & Row, 1940), p. 68.

   33. Frank D. Morris, Reader's Digest, Vol. 35, No. 203, July 1939, p. 55.

   34. Ibid.

4 · *Gearing Up for War*

The network representatives had little reporting to do in the
months following the Munich Crisis. International developments slowed, although it looked as if the Pope would die soon.
CBS did add a third man, however, in the winter of 1938–39.
Paley reports Thomas B. Grandin joined the network in 1938,[1]
although Shirer does not mention him until March 3, 1939, describing him as "Tom Grandin, our Paris correspondent, intel-
ligent but green at radio, having just been hired. . . ."[2]

Grandin's career with CBS was a short one, lasting about
eighteen months. He had broadcast at least twice for CBS before joining the regular staff. A native of Cleveland, he was
thirty-one years old when he joined Murrow and Shirer on CBS's
European team. After graduating from Yale in 1930, Grandin
had gone on to study in Berlin and Paris. By 1938, he was associated with the Geneva Council, a branch of the Rockefeller
Foundation, and his specialty was European radio policies.

After leaving CBS in 1940, Grandin joined the war effort,
serving in the Foreign Broadcasting Intelligence Service. In 1943,
he worked for the United Nations, coordinating monitoring operations. Early in 1944, he returned to foreign correspondence,
this time for NBC's Blue network. In the early summer of that
year, Grandin jumped into Normandy with a group of American paratroopers. He suffered head injuries in an auto accident
in France that summer, and his broadcast career ended.

But in 1939 and the first half of 1940, Grandin was CBS's man
in Paris. Shirer's first contact with Grandin as a CBS staff member was rather strange. Pope Pius XI had died February 12, 1939,
and Shirer had gone to Rome to cover the burial. He returned

to the Vatican in March to cover the election of a new Pope, but had gotten a bad case of the flu en route from Switzerland. Unable to do anything but stay in bed when he got to Rome, Shirer was to be reinforced by Grandin, who came down from Paris. The illness got so bad that Shirer was delirious on March 3 when Grandin arrived. That was also the day that Cardinal Pacelli was elected Pope, and Shirer's instructions for the broadcast made little sense to Grandin, possibly due in part to Grandin's unfamiliarity with radio jargon. "He did gather that I had arranged a broadcast from the balustrade around St. Peter's during the afternoon. He got there, found Father Delancy, who was talking for us, and just as they were signing off, they got a message through their earphones from inside the Vatican to stand by, passed it on to New York, who understood. In a moment they were announcing the name of the new pontiff."[3]

Although there were no major crises in the first part of 1939, it became increasingly difficult for Jordan and Shirer to cover central Europe. Both men had already had enough experience with Nazi censorship to plan broadcasts from "the democracies" whenever possible, with neutral countries, especially Switzerland, the preferred locale. The previous September, Jordan had been refused permission to broadcast from Godesberg without the express permission of the chief of Nazi broadcasting. Jordan had protested that the American airwaves could not be censored. The Nazi replied that orders were orders.

Problems with broadcasting from countries under control of the Third Reich were compounded in March 1939, when French Minister for Foreign Affairs Georges Bonnet instituted censorship on radio foreign correspondence. On March 15, the day Nazi troops occupied Bohemia and Moravia and Hitler declared their annexation to the Reich, Shirer found himself making censorship a priority in deciding how to cover the story. He and Murrow discussed the options over the phone, and although the best information might have been available in Prague or Berlin, it was decided that less information, but more freedom to broadcast what he learned, made Paris a better venue for the report. Ironically, once in France, the new censorship rules meant that Shirer was restricted there, too. He ended up arguing with the French censors over his proposed script into the early hours of the next day.

Two weeks later, as Shirer was overseeing the broadcast of a Hitler speech, the talk was cut off in midsentence on the orders of Hitler himself. Shirer protested, asking at least for an announcement to CBS that the broadcast had been interrupted, but to no avail. White called almost immediately, wanting to know if Hitler had been assassinated. Shirer said no, that he could hear the speech coming into the German studios, so it could be recorded. Later that day, the approved version of the speech was released to Shirer, and he was able to report on its contents.

The impact radio was having on the American public was illustrated for *New York Herald-Tribune* reporter John Elliott after doing several reports from Paris in mid-March as a free-lancer. Elliott received more letters from people who heard his reports on CBS than he ever had in his many years as a newspaper foreign correspondent. The money was pretty good, too, for stringers. Shirer recalls they received fifty dollars a report, which in some cases was more than their weekly salaries.

Shirer went back to the United States in June, sailing on the maiden voyage of the *Mauretania*. In New York, he talked with White, Klauber, and Paley about increasing CBS's foreign coverage, and found that Klauber made most of the significant decisions about news at the network. Murrow had gone back to America in 1938, and both men found that their broadcasts from Europe had made a great impression on the network's listeners. But they also discovered that, contrary to their own beliefs, most Americans doubted that war would come soon, or that it would involve the United States.

In that spring of 1939, there were less than a dozen radio stations in New York City. Most of them did not sign on until 6:30 A.M. and stayed on until midnight or 1 A.M. The Yankee games were on WABC, with "Iron Man" Lou Gehrig's farewell speech just a few months away. The Dodgers were on WOR.

There were fifteen scheduled newscasts during a typical weekday in May 1939, and the broadcasters included Lowell Thomas, Edwin C. Hill, and Gabriel Heatter, not to mention live coverage from Toronto of King George, who was visiting the Dominion. In fact, WJZ, WOR, and WABC had all carried live reports from Canada that day, one of which contained pickups from stations in Commonwealth members around the world.

While in New York, Shirer had a chance to talk at some length with the CBS executives. He even went out to Klauber's country home and sat on a log during one long conversation. With the former *Times* man, Shirer was sure there was an advantage for CBS: "I think it was one reason we had a big advantage because there was no journalist over at NBC (in management) at that time. And Klauber made all the difference in the world because he had been an important journalist for the *New York Times*. It was a lucky break for Paley, and for CBS, and us."[4] Shirer and Murrow also would make a point of seeing Paley when they were in New York, and found him very interested in what they were doing.

Shirer did not return immediately to Geneva when he went back to Europe in the second week of July 1939. He stayed on in London for a meeting with Murrow, Grandin, and White. CBS made no secret of plans to expand the European staff, and had actually released a report to the press about White's trip abroad. The result of the meeting was not much different than previous ones Murrow and Shirer had held.

Figuring that NBC was planning to hire well-known politicians from foreign countries, such as Churchill, Flandin, and Gayda, the CBS men decided to hire Americans. "We think our plan is better. American listeners will want news, not foreign propaganda, if war comes. We are distressed at the failure of the Poles to rush their new shortwave transmitter to completion, as this may leave us in a hole."[5]

Actually, it seems unlikely that NBC planned to replace their representatives, Bate and Jordan, with foreign politicians. Possibly, however, NBC executives were thinking about neutrality and going back to the policy they had used in covering earlier conferences involving world powers. The policy was that the network representatives limit themselves to introducing speakers and let the politicians delineate their positions. Or the politicians might have been seen as "color" men to explain the developments to Americans. Schechter had made it clear that he preferred Americans to string news for NBC, and in any event, the purported plan never went into effect.

NBC was at the time trying to find "someone like Kaltenborn,"[6] to provide the kind of analysis which had captivated CBS patrons the year before. NBC president Lenox Lohr had written RCA chief Sarnoff in April to explain that one reason for the loss of NBC listeners to CBS had been news coverage, including Kaltenborn's broadcasts. The search ended when Kaltenborn left CBS for NBC a year later.

NBC had added another man, Paul Archinard, to assist in Paris. He was an American who had been brought up in France. It is likely that he was initially a stringer for NBC, then went to full-time work after the war began. NBC was still using a stringer from Paris at the start of the war, because Edwin Hartrich, who later worked for CBS, served NBC then. But by October 1, 1939, Schechter listed Archinard as one of NBC's three staff members in Europe.

CBS added one staff member on the eve of the war. Eric Sevareid was hired in late August. He was twenty-six years old and was holding down two jobs when approached by Murrow. During the day, he was city editor of the *Paris Herald*. At night, he worked for the United Press.

Sevareid had come to Europe with his new wife in 1937 to study at the London School of Economics. But soon they went to France, where Sevareid got the *Herald* job. The paper was an English language daily which served the American community there. Newspapering was not new to Sevareid, for he had worked on the *Milwaukee Journal* and before that on high school and college papers. One of his most bitter moments as a youth had been when he was deprived of the editorship of the University of Minnesota school paper because of his liberal political views.

Sevareid had been a foreign correspondent, of sorts, at the age of seventeen when he took a most remarkable trip by canoe with a friend all the way from their home in Minnesota to Hudson Bay in Canada. Along the way he sent reports back to his hometown paper, the *Minneapolis Star*. It was an exhausting trip, lasting from June into the fall, and was recounted in *Canoeing with the Cree*,[7] which has erroneously been called a children's book. The adventure opened Sevareid's eyes to many truths about human nature and mother nature. At one point, the two young men thought of quitting. "I knew instinctively that if I gave up now, no matter what the justification, it would become easier forever afterwards to justify compromise with any achievement."[8]

So they continued on, missing the start of college, but seeing things no white men had seen before. In the next few years, Sevareid saw much of the United States, partly via the hobo highway—America's depression-era train tracks. He even spent one summer panning for gold. Through his experiences on lakes, rivers, and mountains, Sevareid became a physically strong man who carried for a time the nickname "Slim." He was also known as one who could get along with all kinds of folks.

Sevareid gained more exposure to radio as he was growing up than any of the other representatives on the networks' European staffs in 1939. He mentions buying his mother a radio in the early thirties, but as a student who mostly supported himself through school, Sevareid probably had little time for radio listening, and certainly did not have the familiarity Murrow gained with the medium while working in New York. The two men had first met in England while Sevareid was going to the London School of Economics. Sevareid recalls that Murrow was one of a number of journalists he met in his first weeks in England.

I was more sharply impressed, as it happened, by a young American, a tall, thin man with a boyish grin, extraordinary dark eyes that were alight and intense one moment, and somber and lost the next. He seemed to possess that rare thing, an instinctive, intuitive recognition of truth. His name was Edward R. Murrow. He talked about England through half the night, and, although he had been there only a year, one went away with the impulse to write down what he had said, to recapture his phrases, so that one could recall them and think about them later. I knew I wanted to listen to this man again, and I had a strong feeling that many others ought to know him.[9]

The Sevareids soon left for France, and it was not until the late summer of 1939 that Sevareid heard Murrow's voice again.

At the time, Sevareid was pondering a promotion from United Press. But he was also unsure about his future with the wire service. Then Murrow called with a different kind of offer: "I don't know very much about your experience. But I like the way you write and I like your ideas. There's only Shirer and Grandin and myself now, but I think this thing may develop into something. There won't be any pressure on you to provide scoops or anything sensational. Just provide the honest news, and when there isn't any news, why, just say so. I have an idea people might like that." [10]

Sevareid decided to give it a try. An audition, over the entire network, was arranged for the next night. He remembers it as "traumatic, like being on stage in Carnegie Hall with no pants on." [11] Even now, knowing that Shirer and others had difficult times with their auditions, Sevareid marvels that he was hired after the test broadcast. "Mine was pretty lousy. Mine really was. I don't think New York liked the sound of me at all. And Murrow said, 'Well, we'll fix that. You hang around and we'll get you on the payroll.' " [12]

Sevareid's first day on the job was August 22, 1939. He recalls making seventy-five dollars a week to start, which he considered to be a lot of money. Sevareid had started work the day after Hitler signed a nonaggression pact with Russia. It marked the beginning of a period of crisis, in which the possibility of war loomed ever larger. From August 22 to August 29, CBS broadcast eighty-one short wave reports from Europe, NBC, seventy-nine.

Mutual had also augmented its European staff with a regular correspondent from Berlin. Sigrid Schultz was first heard on CBS, but only because Shirer had interviewed her along with several other print reporters as part of a broadcast in September 1938. Soon after that, she started broadcasting for Mutual, doing mostly fifteen-minute reports about once a week.

At that point, Schultz had been a foreign correspondent for twenty years. Along with Peggy Hull, Rheta Childe Door, Sophie Treadwell, Mary O'Reilly, and Maude Radford Warren, she was one of about a dozen female correspondents who reported some part of World War I for print media.

Schultz was born in Chicago, but spent most of her early years in Europe, traveling with her parents. Her father was a successful portrait artist, and he moved the family to Europe permanently in 1911. Schultz graduated from the Sorbonne in 1916 and in 1919 went to be with her family in Berlin, where her father had established a studio. Because of her mother's poor health, the family had to remain in Germany during the war and register as aliens. Schultz got a job as a translator and tutor, monitoring classes at Berlin University for a student who could not speak German. In addition to English, she spoke German, French, Dutch, and Polish.

In late 1919, Schultz became a secretary and assistant to Richard Henry Little, the *Chicago Tribune* correspondent in Berlin. Little was a veteran of world conflicts. He had covered the Spanish-American War, the Russo-Japanese War, and most recently had been with the Allied Expeditionary Force in Europe and the White Army in Russia. Schultz apparently learned about news while she typed Little's letters, because she wrote a number of articles which were published in the *Tribune*. In 1925, she became the paper's correspondent-in-chief for central Europe, a post she kept until 1941.

By the time Schultz was interviewed by Shirer in 1938, she was acknowledged to be an authority on the Nazis. She had first interviewed Hitler in 1931, and had Goebbels over to dinner more than once. In his diary, Shirer wrote that Schultz was "the only woman correspondent in our ranks, buoyant, cheerful, and always well informed."[13]

Schultz was a dedicated reporter for Mutual. In August 1940, she was wounded while rushing to report the effects of one of the first British bombing attacks on Berlin. She continued on to the broadcasting center despite a painful leg injury and did her report, only to find later that technical problems had prevented her broadcast from being heard in America. Schultz left Germany early in 1941 because she contracted typhus, and she went back to America to recover.

But in August 1939, she was reporting frequently for Mutual, and in contrast to the usually shorter reports on NBC and CBS, she often spoke in chunks of ten or fifteen minutes. Recordings show Schultz read her copy at a rapid pace with little pause for emphasis. At times she stumbled, and during one report she broke into giggles over her mistakes. The information was excellent, and she astutely analyzed what was happening in those last days before war. But she wrote like the newspaperwoman she was, and at the beginning of each broadcast she identified herself as the Berlin correspondent of the *Chicago Tribune*.

Censorship was again a major problem for Shirer and Jordan as war approached. Shirer had been blocked from broadcasting from Berlin on August 21. He was able to get through four nights later, although he had expected all radio correspondence from Germany to be halted again. Oddly, with the war just a few days away, the entertainment people at CBS were trying to do a broadcast for later in the week which would feature European dance music from night spots in London, Paris, and Berlin. Shirer and Murrow objected to the proposed program, and it was not broadcast.

On August 25, Britain signed a formal treaty with Poland. The war was postponed while Hitler negotiated directly with the Polish leaders. Then, on August 29, Russia and Germany agreed upon a division of Poland, and war was just a matter of days away. During this time, there were developments almost hourly. As they had been doing during the Munich Crisis a year earlier, Americans were listening to their radios with rapt attention. The audience gained during 1938 had stayed with radio news. A survey of sixteen Indiana counties in July 1939 found that radio was the preferred news source for 67 percent of the respondents. A second survey done at about the same time had shown similarly impressive results.[14]

In his book about the outbreak of war, Raymond Gram Swing noted that world distance had been reduced by radio, even more so than by the airplane. "The change is far too great for its significance to have been sufficiently grasped or to be fully exploited. What this means to the future is hard to define, but it means a great deal in the abstract. The world at this moment, when it is divided by the most destructive forces man has yet contrived, is more united than ever before."[15]

As the last days of August faded, the networks were broadcasting from Europe five and six times a day. H. V. Kaltenborn was there too, and so White had to find a substitute. He came up with Elmer Davis, probably at the urging of Klauber, who had been a friend of Davis's since they had both worked at the *Times*. Starting August 22, Davis was on the air for CBS several times a day, pausing only for the basics of life. After the war began, he stopped to write about the previous three weeks: "For me, and for most people in radio, these nineteen days have been nothing but an endlessly rolling strip of time, punctuated at irregular and unpredictable intervals by brief blank spots of sleep."[16]

On August 31, Shirer did one broadcast from Berlin in which he reported that the situation was very critical, and an hour and a half later he was back on the air giving a simultaneous translation of the Nazi terms for peace in Poland. The next morning he detailed the Nazi attack on Poland, speaking to those who were listening in the small hours of the morning. CBS had gone to a twenty-four-hour broadcast day because of the crisis and maintained it over the next few days.

Murrow had broadcast from London on August 31 that the British government had decided to evacuate children and invalids to the countryside. And Shirer and Murrow also participated in a four-way discussion called a "round table," which may also have included Davis in New York and correspondent Albert L. Warner in Washington. Round tables were done in the previous crises as a variation of the roundup, with the anchorman in New York serving as a sort of master of ceremonies, and the correspondents asking questions of each other after initial reports. The round tables became a regular part of CBS coverage in the first weeks of the war.

Kaltenborn had broadcast from London on August 30, then caught a plane to New York, and went on the air almost immediately after his arrival—forty-one hours after being heard from England. But Davis carried the bulk of the load in New York until Kaltenborn arrived, not leaving the block, which contained his hotel room and the CBS offices, for nine straight days at the end of the month.

When Germany attacked Poland on September 1, 1939, Davis got a call in his hotel room, but it was decided he would not come in until later in the morning, while other CBS announcers handled the predawn talking. When he did go in, Davis found the newsroom bustling with people putting together the pieces from a number of sources. "I looked around the Columbia newsroom, remembering how I had heard of the outbreak of another war in the *New York Times* city room on August 1, 1914; and it struck me that all of the men in the room with the single exception of one of the top executives of the system [probably Klauber] who came down because he was an old newspaper-man and couldn't keep away from the excitement—I was the only one who had worn long pants in 1914. Most of my present colleagues, then, had not even been born." [17]

When England declared war on Germany two days later, CBS called in a full crew at dawn on a Sunday. "I turned on the radio in my room (at the hotel) and took notes on Chamberlain with one hand while I was pulling on my clothes with the other; then got to the office in two minutes, and by the time they had finished reading such early bulletins as had come in I was ready to go on the air." [18]

Jordan had tried to broadcast from Germany when the war began but gave up. He had watched as sand bags were piled up in public places on the night of September 2 and went to Broadcasting House to file his report. In it, Jordan tried to explain to his listeners that they should regard the report differently than those they had heard from Germany before. "American commentators are handicapped just now. There are limitations imposed by the present situation, and more discretion must be used than ever before. All I am saying, therefore, requires a certain reserve." [19]

That opening paragraph was tossed out by the censor, who had lived for several years in the United States, and had even taught college in the Midwest. And so much else of his report was eliminated that Jordan felt it was not even worth broadcasting. It was the first of many skirmishes with the censors in Nazi Germany. Jordan felt that the battle was lost and would have preferred to abandon the bureau there. But NBC decided it was better to keep the option open. Shirer tried to use voice inflection to get his meaning across.

In Paris, Sevareid and Grandin took turns broadcasting in shifts. Sometimes Sevareid would not even get undressed before falling into bed at the end of his "watch." "We were warned over and over again to speak calmly, dispassionately; we must not display a tenth of the emotion that a broadcaster does when describing a prize fight. America was neutral: our company was determined that it would never be guilty of propagandizing Americans into war. This was right, it was the only legitimate way to perform our function—but it was very hard."[20]

A memo had been issued at CBS during the first week of September 1939 establishing those points which the correspondents sought to fulfill. The position was soon adopted by all three networks in a joint statement.

On the day war was declared by Britain and France against Germany, Murrow broadcast the attitude he intended to take in reporting to America. "I have an old-fashioned belief that Americans like to make up their own minds on the basis of all available information. The conclusions you draw are your own affair. I have no desire to influence them and shall leave such efforts to those who have more confidence in their own judgements than I have in mine."[21]

The desire to be neutral in covering the war might have gone all the way back to the beginning of the decade and Paley's discussion of objectivity with Klauber. Paley had restated the original notion in late 1937 that "We must never try to further either side of any debatable question."[22]

The statement all of the networks released after war was declared expanded on that idea: "News analysts are at all times to be confined strictly to explaining and evaluating such fact, rumor, propaganda, and so on, as are available. No news analyst or news broadcaster of any kind is to be allowed to express personal editorial judgment or . . . to say anything in an effort to influence action or opinion of others one way or another."[23]

NBC had taken a stance similar to CBS's at the outbreak of war. It was detailed by Schechter in a magazine article in October 1939: "Knowing full well the responsibility that rests with radio, the NBC news policy called for this war coverage—as well as the crisis coverage of the past—to deal strictly with the facts. Unbiased, unvarnished, responsible facts. Facts shorn of personal feelings, personal thoughts, and personal opinions. Above all, in all news reports, observations, and commentaries, order Number 1 was "No gazing into a crystal ball."[24]As Poland fell, there was even greater desire for neutrality on the part of the networks. NBC and Mutual went so far as to briefly cease broadcasting reports from their men on the European continent.

Shirer and Jordan probably had the most difficullty in holding back their personal feelings about the Nazis. In addition to the constant irritation of censorship, they both commented in their books about the lies in the Nazi media. But Murrow, rather than the Berlin correspondents, seems to have strayed the most from the official policy, revealing his belief that America should do more to help Britain and France.[25]

Murrow, Shirer, and Davis all received letters accusing them of being in the pay of the British government. Perhaps the most amusing was one which claimed that Davis was really a Limey who had trained himself to speak with a phoney Midwestern accent.

Sometimes the effort to be neutral got in the way of good broadcasting. Sevareid and Grandin were chastised by someone in New York because they did not close the windows of the Paris studio while they were on the air, and air raid sirens which started up while they were broadcasting could be heard distinctly in America.

And not all listeners were appreciative of the extensive coverage of European developments. White received a wave of protests when popular programs were interrupted for bulletins or cancelled for special news broadcasts. CBS did, in fact, change their policy so that bulletins were given at the end of programs unless they were of "transcendental importance." However, no one seemed to know what transcendental was, and CBS had been helped in the competition with NBC by breaking into less-popular programs for late-breaking news.

Within three weeks of the start of war, the Poles had been beaten, and the situation settled into a "sit-down" war. CBS and NBC continued to have problems reporting from Germany. Shirer complained, for instance, that both networks were stopped from broadcasting on October 19, 1939, with no explanation.

Despite these problems, in the eighteen months between March 1938 and September 1939, broadcast foreign correspondence, and along with it radio news in America, had been transformed. The radio representatives had gone from being men who primarily secured others to talk, to correspondents who spoke themselves more often than they secured other reporters.

On the American side of the Atlantic, the news staffs at NBC and CBS had been greatly expanded, both in terms of bureaus in important American cities and workers in the network newsrooms in New York. The affiliated stations were paying more attention to news as well, and got used to having network entertainment programs interrupted by bulletins.

News forms for presenting news had been developed, including the roundup and round table, with technical advances accompanying the new methods of reporting. It may be that CBS, using news as an important springboard, had overtaken NBC in that year and a half. *Variety* carried a story which gave the nod for European coverage to the younger network. "CBS gets closer to the human element, and they get to the essentials quickly, interpreting past and present as simply as possible for the ordinary listener."[26]

Sevareid feels that by the fall of 1939, CBS had set itself apart from NBC and Mutual.

We were the first to have our own correspondents day after day, a couple of times a day, same people every day. And the other networks were still using politicians, newspapermen, and others. And that is what gave CBS its jump ahead. Until that time they'd been far behind NBC, which had two networks, and they had gotten the better spots on the dial in most cities. It was the news thing, and the whole country listened to us. And they had to, the others, imitate that. That gave CBS an identity. In fact, the development of news organizations in all of the networks was the thing that gave each network a certain personality and made them distinguishable, one from the other. Otherwise they were collections of paper contracts, with talent here and there, and a bunch of leased cables and telephone wires. That's what a network was. But the news thing was its own thing. So I think it did start with us.[27]

The groundwork had been laid, but many of the broadcasts which would become imprinted on the American consciousness were still to come in the next twelve months, and the innovations which had been made were, importantly, still to be ratified.

NOTES

1. Paley, *As It Happened*, p. 135.

2. Shirer, *Berlin Diary*, p. 158.

3. Ibid., pp. 158–59.

4. Shirer, interview with the author, October 11, 1980.

5. Shirer, *Berlin Diary*, p. 169.

6. Erik Barnouw, *The Golden Web: A History of Broadcastinq in the United States, 1933–1953* (New York: Oxford University Press, 1968), p. 136.

7. Eric Sevareid, *Canoeing with the Cree* (1935; reprint ed., St. Paul: St. Paul Historical Society, 1960).

8. Eric Sevareid, *Not So Wild a Dream* (New York: Knopf, 1941), p. 16.

9. Ibid., p. 82.

10. Murrow, quoted by Sevareid, *Not So Wild a Dream*, p. 107.

11. Cited in Gary P. Gates, *Air Time: The Inside Story of CBS News* (New York: Harper & Row, 1978), p. 40.

12. Sevareid, interview with the author, November 6, 1980.

13. Shirer, *Berlin Diary*, p. 42.

14. Paul W. White, *Covering a War for Radio* (New York: CBS, 1940), p. 2.

15. Raymond Gram Swing, *How War Came* (New York: Norton, 1939), p. 7.

16. Elmer Davis, "Broadcasting the Outbreak of War," *Harper's*, Vol. 179, November 1939.

17. Ibid.

18. Ibid.

19. Jordan, *Beyond All Fronts*, p. 234.

20. Sevareid, *Not So Wild a Dream*, p. 111.

21. F. D. M. Hall (ed.), *This Is London* (New York: Simon & Schuster, 1941), p. 11.

22. *Broadcasting*, December 15, 1937.

23. Sherman Dryer, *Radio in Wartime* (New York: Greenberg, 1942), p. 164.

24. *Current History*, October 1939, p. 36.

25. See Culbert, *News for Everyman*, especially his discussion of Kaltenborn and Murrow; and Barnouw, *The Golden Web*, especially the "Edge of Chaos" chapter.

26. Quoted in Kendrick, *Prime Time*, p. 178.

27. Sevareid, interview with the author, November 6, 1980.

1. CBS News Director Paul White and commentator H. V. Kaltenborn during the Munich Crisis coverage, September 1938. Kaltenborn filled in the gaps from New York while Murrow and Shirer reported from Europe. Photo courtesy of CBS.

2. Thomas B. Grandin, Edward R. Murrow, and William L. Shirer (*top to bottom*), probably in July 1939, upon landing in Paris for a meeting on future coverage for CBS. Photo courtesy of CBS.

3. NBC Correspondent Fred Bate, *top left*, who was based in London; NBC Paris Correspondent Paul Archinard, *top right*; and NBC European Correspondent Max Jordan, *bottom*. Pictures taken in June 1939. Photo courtesy of The National Broadcasting Company, Inc.

4. Edward R. Murrow, Mary Marvin Breckinridge, and William L. Shirer (*left to right*) being fitted for skates on a Dutch canal in January 1940. Photo courtesy of Mary Marvin Breckinridge (Mrs. Jefferson Patterson).

5. CBS Athens Bureau Chief Betty Wason listens in on radio for news of the war, spring of 1940. The uniform was custom-made since the male correspondents were issued uniforms. Photo courtesy of Betty Wason.

6. Margaret Rupli, who reported for NBC from Holland in early 1940, taken shortly after she returned to the United States after escaping the Nazi invasion. Photo courtesy of Margaret Rupli Woodward.

7. Helen Hiett and NBC News Director Abe Schechter admiring National
Headliners Club Award she received for reporting on the attack on Gibraltar in
late 1940. Photo courtesy of The National Broadcasting Company, Inc.

5 · Adding to the Core

In the first few weeks of the war, network correspondents traveled even more than before to check the changes in the people and places of Europe. Murrow did not go far, but he did go often—prowling around London, testing the mood, working off his own nervousness. He must have had a good sense of direction as well, at one point taking a tour of southern London after all of the identifying street signs had been removed. He did not get lost once.

He also entertained, or was entertained, frequently, with a good number of dinner parties on the calendar. "Murrow was a familiar figure in London and was eagerly sought out by members of Parliament, ministers of state, and leaders of exiled governments, some of whom he and his wife Janet entertained in their small apartment."[1]

When he did report, Murrow began to show the style which would make him the number one newsman in America a year later. Edward Bliss wrote in introducing a collection of Murrow's scripts: "Murrow's early shortwave reports from London were prototypes of all his broadcasts of the war years to come: what is happening, how does it relate to the American, how does common man feel."[2]

Shirer would often use public transit as a source for his reports. He would listen to conversations of fellow travelers to get a sense of the public mood. Of course, this was also partially a necessity, because he could not obtain enough rationed gas to operate his car.

Both Shirer and Murrow were aware of sociology, and mentioned it by name, Murrow claiming at one point to be a rather poor sociologist. In another broadcast, he discussed British class consciousness, and related how the long hours in bomb shelters were wearing some of it away.

All of the correspondents read newspapers, of course, and in their broadcasts they frequently made reference to something they had read. They also listened to the radio, both domestic programs and shortwave ones. Jordan had some advantage over the others because he knew people all over Europe from his multinational childhood and could speak more languages. He had also been a member of a luncheon club which met every Friday at a Berlin restaurant. Like some of Murrow's meals, these luncheons could provide good material for Jordan.

There were also the usual beat rounds to make—the embassies, government departments, and even public relations agencies were occasionally good for a broadcast or two. Shirer, for example, was invited to a Lufthansa tea at which Lindbergh gave a talk.

Sevareid kept on the move that fall, first going north from Paris to see the Allied Expeditionary Force land. He slipped away from Paris on September 10, along with a correspondent from the *London Daily Express*, Geoffrey Cox, and went to Cherbourg. They were the only two journalists to see the troops come ashore, and Sevareid got a good broadcast out of it, except the censors would not let him say how the men had landed, which seemed pretty silly to him. "It was a remarkable censorship in those days. It was either so ruthless that it cut out the most harmless observations, or so inefficient that one could pass the most sensational news. It operated entirely by whim and caprice, and one never knew from day to day how his dispatches would fare."[3]

On September 17, Sevareid and three print foreign correspondents went to the battle lines near the Luxembourg border. They had not received specific instructions not to travel, and the four reporters were not willing to wait for the French to set up tours to the front. They managed to pass through a number of check points, and got close enough to the front lines to find there was almost no fighting.

Back in Paris, Sevareid was preparing his script on the trip when he and his fellow travelers got a scare. The other correspondents who had stayed behind got wind of the trip, and fearing they would be scooped, one of them imitated a French official and said the quartet would be expelled if they filed their stories. The hoax was exposed an hour after it was played, and Sevareid filed his "all quiet" story. The wayward reporters did receive a lecture from the real authorities, but no permanent restrictions were put on them.

It is interesting to note that Sevareid reported what he had seen at the front to the American Embassy military authorities. They were not allowed to see the front for themselves. Jordan also may have passed information along to American diplomats; this is indicated by a curious line in his account of the German occupation of Denmark. Having been tipped off that Germany was mobilizing for invasion, Jordan went to Copenhagen and wired NBC that he was on to a big story. The next day, two days before the invasion, Jordan went to see a friend at the American Legation. In an apparent attempt to explain his action then, Jordan wrote later: "The United States, it must be remembered, was then still a neutral, and I realized that I as an American citizen, had to exercise the utmost caution in planning my moves. At the same time, of course, it was my duty to make proper use of important information in my possession." [4] Exactly what that duty was is not explained.

Competition continued to fire Jordan in the time between the fall of Poland and the next blitzkrieg through Scandinavia. In late November, he beat Shirer on news of Russia's invasion of Finland by tying up the German transmitter and obtaining exclusive rights initially to the Finnish government statements. But Shirer, with advice from Murrow and help from BBC engineers, rigged a pickup from the north which turned out to be better than NBC's. And eventually, CBS obtained equal access to the Finnish decrees. Shirer had a terrible case of the flu while this was happening. Spurred by orders from New York to "get the broadcasts," he did, but the phone and cable bill for two days was $1,500.

Murrow made his first excursion with British forces during November. Against the wishes of White, he went on board a minesweeper in the North Atlantic. Fred Bate was also on the trip, and their friendship grew as the two men were repeatedly teamed up on similar expeditions. The British were determined to show impartiality to the foreign broadcasters, and equal access was one way of doing that.

On December 13, Shirer found himself in competition with Jordan again. This time it was an interview with the captain of the German ship *Bremen*, which had run a British blockade along the coast of Norway. "Jordan and I scrapping as to who shall have the radio interview with Commodore Ahrens, the *Bremen's* skipper. I do not like this kind of competition. By scrapping we play right into Nazi hands."[5]

The Germans wanted to provide the interview to both networks, but with the questions asked by Lothrop Stoddard, an American who wrote white supremist literature. Shirer objected to the Propaganda Ministry naming his interviewers and rejected the arrangement.

Three days before, he had felt more kindly toward the Nazi media policy, as he and Murrow had participated in a round table—the first time he had talked with Murrow since phone lines between London and Berlin had been disconnected at the start of war. "So that we would not give information of benefit to the enemy, we worked out our conversation in advance. I submitted my questions and Ed's answers as well as his questions and my answers beforehand to the Germans and he doing the same with the British. Both sides proved very decent about the whole script."[6]

One of the biggest stories of December came not from Europe but from Uruguay. A German battleship, the *Graf Spee*, had been cruising the South Atlantic, preying on commercial shipping. At least nine ships had been sunk. The British sent three cruisers after the *Graf Spee* and found it on December 13 off the coast of Uruguay. Following a running battle of fourteen hours, the Germans made for the neutral port of Montevideo and reached it safely on the fourteenth.

James Bowen, a stringer for NBC, "the only reporter who had a microphone and a shortwave transmitter at his command," described the last stages of the battle and the events which followed.[7] After burying thirty-six sailors who had died in the sea battle and putting wounded in a Montevideo hospital, the Germans started repairing the ship and stocking up on supplies.

On December 15, the Uruguayan authorities gave the ship's captain two days to leave port or be interned. On the evening of the December 17, while several hundred thousand Uruguayans watched, the ship was deliberately sunk in the harbor, apparently on direct orders from Hitler.

In Berlin, Shirer was amused to listen to his radio and hear both the British and the Germans claim victory in the incident. When the commander of the *Graf Spee* committed suicide in Buenos Aires on December 20, Shirer noted that the German people were told the captain went down with his ship.

CBS's newest foreign correspondent took her post in December 1939. Marvin Breckinridge was the first female correspondent on CBS, and like the half dozen other women who broadcast for the networks during the war, her career on radio was relatively short compared to those of Jordan, Murrow, Sevareid, and Shirer.

Breckinridge had been on the same ship in April 1937 which carried Ed and Janet Murrow to their new assignment in London. She had gone to England with her parents to witness the royal transition. Her parents had seen the crowning of King George VI's father, George V, over a quarter of a century before. They were frequent travelers to Europe, and Breckinridge had been to Europe three times herself while still a child.

The Breckinridges were a prominent family. As a child, their daughter was called Mary Marvin, but two older relatives with the first name of Mary became so well known that she switched to Marvin as a teenager. Her social debut was made at age eighteen in New York, and she was also presented at court in London. By then (1926) she was majoring in history and modern languages at Vassar College and was active in national and international student groups.

Breckinridge became president of the National Student Federation in 1927, and attended conferences in the late 1920s in Copenhagen, Prague, Rome, Paris, and Budapest. By the time she graduated, Breckinridge was conversant in a handful of foreign languages and was considering a career in the foreign service. Instead of doing that, however, she renewed a childhood interest in photography and studied at the Clarence White

School in New York. She directed, produced, and shot a motion picture called *The Forgotten Frontier* in 1929–30. It was about the Frontier Nursing Service of rural Kentucky, which had been founded by a cousin.

Breckinridge had begun photographing before she was ten. A vest pocket Kodak that was a birthday present started her on a New York shooting spree. "I rode the top of a bus all down Fifth Avenue to Washington Square and took photographs of the Metropolitan Museum and the Public Library and Washington Arch. I still have them and they're simply terrible, but I've loved photography ever since."[8]

Breckinridge's increasing success as a professional photographer in the 1930s meant she could go pretty much where she wanted in the world and be able to sell photos to American magazines. When she went to Europe in the summer of 1939, Breckinridge was warned that war would soon break out. But with commitments for a photo story on the Lucerne Music Festival and another on the Nuremberg Nazi Rally, she went ahead. "I was staying at a hotel in Lucerne for the music festival but the news got worse and worse. When the Germans marched into Poland I realized that it meant war, and the kinds of things I came to do were silly. It was wartime."[9]

She headed for London and arrived the night before war was declared. Breckinridge considered returning to the United States and then thought about volunteering to be an ambulance driver in England. Deciding to go home, she went down to the London office of the American Express to buy a ticket. She found Picadilly Circus and the Haymarket crowded with Americans trying to book passage home and decided she did not need to rush back.

Instead, Breckinridge went to the Fleet Street office of Black Star, an international photo agency whose New York office already represented her. Most British photographers had been mobilized, so Breckinridge got work immediately. And her shooting subject played a part in her radio debut. "I'd been doing a piece on an English village preparing for war, and another one on slum children being moved to the country, and Ed and Janet just asked me to dinner one night. We were just chatting, and he asked me to talk about it on the air that Saturday night."[10]

Before going on the air with her, Murrow offered two sug-
gestions to the newcomer. He thought it was a good idea for
Breckinridge to use her full name, and advised her to keep her
voice low. Murrow saw her home and promised a check, which
never came.

But she did start getting phone messages a few days later to
call Murrow. He wanted her to spend a night in the city of
London in a firehouse which was staffed by women. Breckinridge agreed, and a week after her first report to America, she
told CBS listeners about the female fire-fighting force, which had
little work at that point in the war.

Breckinridge had planned to visit Ireland at some point in her
stay, so she asked Murrow if he would use a report on the Irish
neutrality—strange in view of traditional ties to England. The
Irish broadcast went so well that Murrow immediately asked
her to return to London so she could pack up for a European
assignment. It turned out to be Holland.

Breckinridge made her first broadcast from Holland on December 10, as part of *The World This Week*. It was a Sunday
broadcast, and was typical of appearances by female broadcasters for both networks; they were often shunted to the weekend
reports and never led off a roundup. This particular one started
with Shirer from Berlin reporting on some concentration camp
escapees who had been caught and hanged. Warren Sweeney,
a network announcer in New York, followed with information
about Russian protests against Britain's blockade of Germany.
Then Sevareid came in from Paris. He had been on a tour of
the Maginot Line and told about the French defenses there.
Murrow gave details released in London on fighting between
German and British troops on the Continent. Breckinridge was
the final correspondent in the broadcast, telling about Dutch
preparations for war.

When Breckinridge arrived in Holland, she did not know how
many reports she would be making. She could not even tell the
hotel clerk how long she would be staying at the Carlton, where
most of the journalists hung out. On December 21, she broadcast again, telling of the gathering horde of foreign correspondents in Holland and then about the Dutch frontier defenses.
Part of her reconnaissance had been done by bicycle.

The foreign correspondents all played a part in the networks'

Christmas broadcasts. Jordan did one from the Siegfried Line, featuring a lot of Christmas cheer but little fighting. NBC also had one from the Maginot Line, probably done by Archinard. Sevareid was there along the Maginot Line too, but a technician in either Paris or New York turned the wrong switch and not a word from France was heard in America, especially not the cursing which followed when Sevareid found that the weeks of work he and Grandin had done setting up the broadcast had been for naught.

Shirer was to have been along the Siegfried Line for his Christmas broadcast, but Jordan obtained it first, and apparently only one person could do it from there. Considering himself to have been double-crossed by the Nazis, he stopped his evening broadcasts for a week in protest—certainly a curious tactic, but not unlike the BBC's approach to foreign attempts at censorship a decade earlier. A substitute broadcast was arranged in time for the holiday.

Early Christmas morning in Berlin, Shirer left a party at the home of friends to do a broadcast as part of CBS's Christmas Eve programming. After a few hours of sleep, he was off to Kiel to broadcast how German sailors were celebrating the holiday. He found nearly the entire German fleet there and also saw a ship in dry dock which the British claimed to have sunk. Since few foreigners had been allowed so close to the fleet, Shirer got considerably more information than if he had been where Jordan was.

Murrow also arranged for an unusual broadcast, again because the usual kind was stymied by the war. Dismayed that wartime broadcast restrictions robbed him of even saying what the Christmas weather was like in London, he set up a shortwave talk between the friends with whom he and Janet Murrow were sharing Christmas dinner, the Macadams, and their two young children in the United States. Ivison Macadam was a Scotsman who was a top official in the British Ministry of Information. His wife, though, was an American, and their children had been sent to live in Portland, Oregon, during the war.

Janet Murrow was a frequent participant in holiday broadcasts. She had made her debut on Thanksgiving Day, 1939, and would appear so often on holidays that she called her role "a kind of greeting card." But later on in the war she did become a correspondent. She possessed a very good speaking voice and a reporter's eye for news.

My beat was hospitals. I was planning to go with the invasion, with one of the field hospitals to France, but Ambassador Winant (U.S. ambassador to Great Britain) persuaded me that he had a job for a person who knew England well. And he said "Look at all the people who want to go with the invasion. They won't have any trouble filling your place." And I never will know whether it was partly that I was scared at the thought of it, or whether I felt I really could do a better job in England. Anyhow, I didn't do any more broadcasting after that. It was a very minor thing, and I obviously got in the back door because Ed was there.[11]

But the broadcast most remembered from Europe that Christmas was made by William L. White. It was done from the Finnish front, the Mannerheim Line, and inspired Robert Sherwood's play "There Shall Be No Night." The report was carried on CBS.

By the end of December, CBS was claiming a dozen correspondents in Europe, and NBC at least four. A few of them were little more than stringers, while several had full staff status. White listed his European staff on January 1, 1940, as: Murrow in London, Shirer in Berlin, Sevareid in Paris, Grandin in Bucharest, William L. White in Helsinki, Breckinridge in Rotterdam, Betty Wason in Stockholm, Cecil Brown in Rome, Russell Hill in Berlin, Erland Echlin in London, and Bill Henry and Larry Lesueur in the field with the French Army.

Several months earlier, Schechter had listed his foreign staff as: Bate in London, Archinard in Paris, and Jordan in central Europe.

Bill Henry began reporting for CBS in the summer of 1939. He was a correspondent for the *Los Angeles Times* and had been for two decades. At the start of the war he was with the RAF in France and also carried a pretty heavy broadcasting load with CBS. That winter he was called back to Los Angeles and resumed his print career stateside.

Erland Echlin was a backup reporter for CBS in London. He rarely broadcast, and Larry Lesueur, who worked with Murrow in London, thinks he was a part-timer. His association with CBS was brief and there is little evidence of any journalistic impact he made.[12]

Russell Hill started working for CBS in September 1939. He was twenty-one years old at the time and had just graduated from Columbia University. On his way to graduate work at Cambridge, Hill decided to spend the summer in Europe and landed a temporary job at the Berlin bureau of the *New York Herald Tribune*. The job lasted until the last week of August, and Hill then took off on his bicycle for Vienna. He was there when the war started and then went on to Budapest. He sent a wire to Joseph Barnes, the *Herald Tribune* bureau chief, asking for the job back. It turned out that the assistant Hill had filled in for was leaving. There was only one problem. The job was his, but Hill would have to get to Berlin on his own. The German counsel in Budapest was not going to grant a visa, until Hill waived the telegram from Barnes and claimed it stated that the paper wanted Hill back in Berlin immediately.

Hill was young even by the standards of the rest of the foreign correspondents, who were mostly in their late twenties. But he recalls that most of the reporters treated him very well and kind of saw him as a prodigy. He had gotten the part-time job with Shirer through Barnes, who was a good friend of Shirer. Hill worked for both men and ran the *Herald Tribune* bureau when Barnes returned to America. He had originally gotten twenty-five dollars a week from the paper and fifty dollars from CBS. The combined salary was positively princely for the new graduate. And when he was acting bureau chief, the pay totaled one hundred dollars. Hill was expelled from Germany because of an article another reporter for the paper wrote in the summer of 1940. The bureau was shut down, and Hill went to Budapest, where he did some reporting for CBS while filing for the paper. But in midsummer, he was sent on to Bucharest, where CBS already had someone, so that effectively ended Hill's broadcasting career. After an extensive career as a print foreign correspondent, Hill went to work for his current employer, Radio Free Europe.

Lawrence E. Lesueur was a full-time staff member, alternating between London and France. Born in June 1909, he was thirty years old when he left United Press in New York in the fall of 1939. His family had a long association with journalism; a grandfather had been a newspaper publisher in Iowa, and his father, a foreign correspondent for the *New York Tribune*. After Henry left the RAF for the United States Lesueur covered the Advanced Air Striking Force in France. He was in Paris for a broadcast on Christmas, 1939.

Cecil Brown was thirty-two years old when he first began reporting for CBS in 1940. He had graduated from Ohio State University in 1929 and saw a bit of the world as a seaman for the next year or so. He started working for United Press in 1931 in Los Angeles and then put in a brief stint as editor of the Prescott, Arizona, *Journal-Miner* in 1933. Brown then headed east, working for the *Pittsburgh Press*, the *Newark Ledger*, and then the *New York American*, before leaving for Europe in 1937.

Brown sailed on *The American Farmer*, going in the lowest class for $105. He arrived in England on October 2, 1937. Brown had decided to go to Europe after the *American* went out of business, and he worked for about two months before he departed as a log keeper on a midnight to 8 A.M. shift. "Since I had that relationship with CBS, however tenuous it was, I went to the CBS office in London when I got there, and I met a man that I'd never really heard of and didn't know, Ed Murrow."[13]

Brown got quite a surprise during that visit. Murrow showed him a box-shaped object with a screen in it and said "That's television." They were looking at a BBC test of the device. Brown remembers that Murrow was "very impressive, a very handsome guy, a very nice person, and very gracious."[14] Nothing was mentioned about a job. Murrow had only just hired Shirer, and Brown does not think Murrow even remembered their earlier meeting when he finally was hired.

After leaving London, Brown traveled for five months, personally viewing most of the spots where trouble was brewing. He got a job early in 1938 with the International News Service in Rome. Brown spoke little Italian, was getting fifty dollars a week, and would soon be married to his childhood sweetheart who came over to join him. Marriage resulted in a raise to sixty-five dollars a week, and he later wrote a weekly "Letter from Rome" for *Newsweek*, which added twenty-five dollars more.

When the print reporters were forbidden to do any more broadcasts for CBS, Brown told Murrow that if the network wanted any more broadcasts from Rome, they would have to come from a correspondent, and he asked for the job. Murrow hired him for one hundred dollars a week. Brown's first broadcast was every bit as traumatic as Shirer's and Sevareid's had been. He even accepted the mispronunciation of his own name and continued to say it that way as long as he broadcast.

Betty Wason was not a CBS staff member at the end of 1939, and she was barely a stringer in the first few months of 1940. She had a working agreement with CBS, but they had not been using her much at all during the winter. Wason had originally gone to Europe in 1938 to see the world and, before leaving America, had obtained press credentials from a Transradio executive. "I simply went in to see Herb Moore and said I was going to Europe and I'd like to be their correspondent. I had been to a lot of places, and by this time, in addition to experience I had been on the staff of *McCall's* magazine. I had copies of a column that had appeared in the *Lexington Herald* for which I was not paid. So here I have newspaper, radio, and magazine experience presumably, so that made me bold enough to say I could be a correspondent."[15]

Wason had grown up in Delphi, Indiana, and started college at Oberlin before transferring to Purdue, where she received her B.A. in Home Economics in 1933 at the age of twenty-one. She then had a series of jobs—an amazing number considering it was the middle of the Depression. In two years she was, among other things, a copywriter, secretary, store clerk, and home economist. When the Kentucky Utilities Company laid off all its home economists, Wason landed a job on WLAP in Lexington. "I put on a cooking demonstration in a corner of a warehouse loft, and local women could come and have a luncheon, and they paid 25 cents a plate. Their club got 15 cents back in a refund. With the remaining 10 cents I put on a luncheon."[16]

Wason had to buy the food and do most of the cooking. She found that women from the local college would serve the lunch for a dollar if they also got a free meal. The demonstration was broadcast over WLAP, and it gave Wason a lot of ad-libbing experience. She soon moved on to a larger station in Cincinnati but was fired within a week when she learned the hard way that she was a much better extemporaneous speaker than a scripted one. That's how she felt she learned how to write for the ear instead of for the eye.

From Ohio, Wason went to New York, where she became an assistant food editor at *McCall's*. In 1936, she joined a public relations firm and set a personal record for longevity on a job by remaining with Raymond C. Mayer until 1938, when she decided to go to Europe. "I began with 300 dollars and a one-way ticket, and credentials from Transradio Press Service without any guarantee of income. I went to Czechoslovakia and was having a great time. I wasn't really serious about any of this. I was there when the Munich Crisis developed, and this is how I became a foreign correspondent, by being in the right place at the right time, and learning that I had a natural instinct for what news is." [17]

Transradio had issued credentials to young people like Wason for just such occasions as the Munich Crisis. The wages were rather modest—twenty-five dollars a week if the reporter was producing material regularly—but Wason remembers getting by on a dollar a day for a hotel room and about the same for food. She found the men covering the crisis to be very helpful at first, but when she became competitive as a journalist, they stopped being so cooperative.

After Munich and the ensuing conference in Vienna, things quieted down in Europe. Wason found that she just was not generating enough income to stay there, and in early 1939, she returned to America. The new New York paper *PM* was being organized then, and she did some work planning the food section but ultimately decided her opportunities were better in Europe because of the Depression lingering on in the United States.

Before leaving, Wason stopped by CBS and talked to White. He had a policy of letting the men in Europe do the hiring but suggested that Wason see Shirer in Berlin. She did that in January 1940, on her way to Scandinavia, and when the invasion of Norway began, Shirer called. "I was down to one Swedish krona, which was the equivalent of twenty-five cents, and I had a room in the Grand Hotel and I had tried everything and I thought 'What am I going to do? There's a war on and I still can't get anything.' I was literally weeping in my hotel room when a call came from Bill Shirer asking me to make a broadcast, and I hurriedly found a girl who could translate from the Swedish papers, and my first broadcast was a scoop."[18]

Wason did have a knack for telling a story in an appealing way, as a transcript of her report shows. "A Swede who had fled from the Swedish Legation in Oslo, along with the rest, was standing by his car outside the house where the court and government were staying, when he saw a German plane coming. He gave the one and only air-raid alarm with his automobile horn. Down the road ran King Haakon, Crown Prince Olaf, the Bitish and Polish Ministers, and all the other governments' officials. They had to stand waist-deep in snow beneath fir strees while bombs crashed."[19]

Wason followed the first broadcast with more reports on the fighting in Norway. She went from Stockholm to a point deep inside Norway near the skirmishing and interviewed wounded British soldiers recuperating in a dance hall which had been taken over by medics.

Another female voice had been added to the foreign correspondence from Europe in the first months of 1940. Margaret Rupli had been hired by NBC to report from Holland in January. The wife of British newspaperman David Woodward, she had been looking for almost any kind of work when she called the American Legation in Amsterdam. By chance, Jordan had called the legation looking for someone who might serve as a reporter for NBC. Rupli got in touch and took a voice test at the Dutch broadcasting facility in Hilversum. Although she had little formal training in journalism, Rupli did possess a strong voice. Her husband used to tease her that even if the broadcast lines were down, her voice could be heard in America anyway.

Short on experience, Rupli's strong suit was a working knowledge of Europe. She had first gone there as a junior in college, studying for a year at the University of Paris before returning to Goucher College, a small liberal arts school outside Washington, D.C. She had graduated Phi Beta Kappa in 1931.

Wanting to study international relations firsthand, Rupli got a job as a one-hundred-dollar-a-month researcher in Geneva for the National Council for the Prevention of War and the Geneva Research Center. In 1934, at the age of 24, Rupli returned to the Untied States and worked for the next three years at the Departement of Labor's Bureau of Labor Statistics. Because she spoke several foreign languages, she also did some translating for the department.

Combining her two interests, Rupli began a Ph.D. program at the University of Chicago in 1937. But the war and romance got in the way, and she returned to Europe in 1939 and married Woodward, whom she had first met in Switzerland six years before. He was assigned to Berlin after they were married, but the war situation caused the *News Chronicle* management to shift his assignment to Amsterdam.

Rupli had initially proposed three topics for broadcast after she was hired at a rate of twenty-five dollars for short pieces (under seven minutes) and fifty dollars for longer ones. And she informed Jordan that she would be using her maiden name in her broadcasts, because that was the one by which she was known in America.

Before she ever broadcast, Rupli received some expert instruction from an unexpected source. In an effort to get CBS's new Holland correspondent settled, Murrow had gone to Amsterdam in January. He also wanted to meet with Shirer in neutral territory. Murrow saw Rupli in the hotel where the correspondents gathered and called her over to where he and Breckinridge were. "Oh, you're the opposition, right? But come here, I'll teach you, too. I hope I'll remember this, too. When you report the invasion of Holland or I report the invasion of England, understate the situation. Don't say the streets are rivers of blood. Say that the little policeman I usually say hello to every morning is not there today."[20]

Murrow and Shirer did a joint broadcast with Breckinridge taking them out to the government broadcasting facilities east of Amsterdam. It was snowing when they got back, and the trio had a little fun throwing snowballs at each other. Another outing in those few days of relative relaxation involved an ice-skating trip along a canal. Breckinridge took along a camera, and there is a photo of the three of them being fitted for skates.

During that outing, Shirer asked Murrow for some time off. His wife and young daughter were living in Switzerland, and he wanted to visit them before the spring thaw and the resumption of serious fighting. Murrow said yes and asked Breckinridge if she would fill in for Shirer in Berlin. She agreed but, before leaving for Germany, did one more broadcast on the severe winter and its effect on Holland's defense system.

When Breckinridge arrived in late January, Shirer gave her an orientation, which included a late night trip to the Rundfunk studios on the Kaiserdamm.

The first night I arrived he took me out with him when he went out to broadcast. We stayed at the Adlon Hotel, which the Germans very kindly let be heated. They wanted to keep the journalists happy, and it was terribly cold that winter, like 12 degrees above zero. And you'd walk, I think, eight steps and feel to the right, and that was the entrance to the subway. There was a glimmer of light there. You'd ride the subway a long way to the Rundfunk office building where the censors were, and get off at Adolf Hitlerplatz, in deep snow with high piles everywhere. Then you turned sharp right across the street and went in again. A German soldier and his police dog were there, and he'd say "Ausweis Bitte—Your pass please," and then once inside Shirer introduced me to everybody and I shook hands with censors and all different kinds of people. He introduced me around beautifully and then we went back at one or two in the morning; the underground trains were still running.[21]

Shirer also took his substitute to introduce her to contacts at the American Embassy, the German Foreign Office, and the German Propaganda Ministry—all sources of news for a foreign correspondent. Shirer also offered some advice for dealing with the Nazi censors. "He told me as an example what he had done the day before. When he described Hitler's birthday, he reported that he had been on Wilhelmstrasse and saw "about 60 persons massed in front" of the Reich's headquarters. That went through the German censor, but anyone knows that sixty persons is not a mass."[22]

Breckinridge had underlined passages in her scripts in Holland so she would remember which words to emphasize. That could not be done in Berlin because of possible problems with censors, but like Shirer, who was a master at using vocal inflection to make a point, Breckinridge mentally underlined her scripts while in Berlin. At times, censors rejected scripts entirely. One time a censor added to her script, writing in a whole sentence. She accepted it "because it did not falsify the story." In addition to the censors at the Propaganda Ministry, there were also ones at the Foreign Office and Defense Ministry. And when Breckinridge did a broadcast on the women's movement in Germany, it required the approval of four censors, the extra one belonging to an agency overseeing women's affairs.

Shirer had been planning to return in February, but he got the flu and did not get back until March. During the six weeks she was filling in for him, Breckinridge was on the air with some frequency. One report was an exclusive interview with the captain of the *Altmark*. The German freighter had been hit by British shells near Norway, and the captain had deliberately run it aground. The "cargo" of the freighter was primarily 303 British seamen who had been taken prisoner after their merchant ships were sunk by the German pocket battleship *Graf Spee*. Like most interviews done under censorship, the questions and answers were written out in advance.

She also found time for socializing in Berlin, and saw quite a bit of Jefferson Patterson, who was in charge of the prisoner-of-war section of the American Embassy. As a representative of a neutral country, he inspected POW camps and judged whether the Geneva treaty was being followed. They had known each other in America, but now Patterson began a courtship by inviting Breckinridge to the opera. By the time she returned to Holland, the couple had decided to get married.

NBC had a fourth correspondent in Europe by 1940. But William Kerker[23] was not full-time. Hill recalls that Kerker assisted him at the *Herald Tribune* office and also worked for NBC. Kerker was in his twenties, and basically assisted in such tasks as reviewing local papers for news. Harry Flannery, who replaced Shirer in Berlin in late 1940, found Kerker to be one of two NBC men in Berlin, the other being Ted Knauth, probably a part-timer too. "Kerker was a tall, handsome, perfectly dressed, dark-haired young man, with an unusually good voice, who had been a student for many years and who spoke perfect German."[24]

As well as the addition of a number of staff members over

the winter of 1939–40, there were other sources of information from Europe available to the networks and to the American public in general. Both CBS and NBC had set up listening stations in America. The receiving sets were located on Long Island. The shortwave broadcasts from Europe were monitored for CBS by specialists sitting in a room on the seventeenth floor of the network offices in Manhattan, not far from the newsroom. Paul White described the operation:

In what we call Listening Room A, loudspeakers range along the ceiling and there are recording machines and transcribers and head-phone sets and typewriters—all the paraphernalia of this job of recording and "sampling" the short wave broadcasts of the warring nations. From the listening room, two lines run directly to a shack out at Roosevelt, L.I. In this shack sits a CBS engineer with the receiving sets banked up in front of him and with a forest of antennae strung up from the tall radio towers outside. Working from a schedule of times and frequencies, he tunes in the shortwave broadcasts from Sydney to Saigon, from Martinique to Montevideo, from Berlin to Brazzaville.[25]

White, with the help of CBS's military commentator, Major George Fielding Elliot, decided the monitoring priorities. First, the four-man crew would tune into regularly scheduled news and propaganda broadcasts. Then they would listen to stations in cities where fighting or other developments were occurring in hopes of hearing any special announcements. Any leftover monitoring time was spent roving the dial listening for anything new, which is how Lord Hee Haw was first heard on the German transmissions. When an extraordinary development was monitored, it could be translated and transmitted to the CBS studio in sixty seconds, and more routine developments took from four to ten minutes.

The listening station staff, understanding about a dozen languages, was supposed to ferret out the news from the 100,000 words a day coming into the center. In addition to using it in their own broadcasts, CBS staffers also sent the significant contents to papers and wire services on a leased line.

Of course, the public had the same opportunity to listen in on shortwave broadcasts as the NBC and CBS operators did. CBS did a survey in 1940 and found that 45 percent of the

American public owned shortwave sets and that 17 percent listened at least once a week. A survey in Baton Rouge found that over 15 percent of the residents there were shortwave listeners and 14 percent had heard German broadcasts. Paul Lazarsfeld found in Erie County, Ohio, that 36 percent of the population owned receivers and over 10 percent listened to news regularly on them. Regarding reception, the BBC broadcasts were judged the clearest, with the German RRGs second.[26]

A study done by the American Institute of Public Opinion for the Princeton Listening Center about the same time found that a third of adult Americans had access to a working shortwave receiver, and that over 10 percent had tuned into a European broadcast the month before. The later figure was questioned because the pollsters felt some respondents had confused rebroadcasts of foreign programs on American commercial stations, such as Mutual's use of BBC reports, with shortwave broadcasts directly received from Europe. The total audience for the broadcasts was estimated at three to seven million, with 150,000 people a day listening to the RRG.[27]

The Nazi offerings for English-speaking people included Lord Hee Haw, a former British Socialist named William Joyce who had split with the British socialist movement and gone to Germany before the war. He had a wide audience, and Sevareid and Murrow both report that they listened to him.

In America, Lord Hee Haw was heard mostly in the afternoon and had relatively little impact compared to his following in Britain. His Oxford-accented broadcasts from the Hamburg station were listened to by so many people there that jokes and songs soon sprang up about him, and a revue at the Holborn Empire Theatre in London in the spring of 1940 was titled "Haw Haw."[28] It featured a stripper and vocalists, one of whom sang a song with these lyrics:

> We've seen ups and downs on the land and the seas,
> We've seen a fan dance and we've seen a strip tease,
> We've seen better things than Lord Haw Haw in trees.[29]

A man identified as E. B. Ward was first monitored on the RRG by the CBS shortwave listening team in January 1940. His

reports included broadcasts from the French front and his comments were at times preceded by a disclaimer stating that he
was an objective reporter. "Ward" was identified by *Time* as fifty-
nine-year-old Edward Leopold Delaney, a sometimes actor and
writer in the United States. Shirer wrote that Delaney "broadcast Nazi propaganda without question." After Italy entered the
war, Ward was even heard on the Facist program "The American Hour," which came nightly from Radio Roma and also featured comments of Ezra Pound on occasion.

Some of the Nazi programs were prepared especially for North
American listeners. "Paul Revere" was a name used by a man
whose broadcasts took the form of letters he read back to his
friends in Iowa. He pictured himself as a German-born American who had married a German girl, and while claiming dual
allegiance, he decided to live in Germany. He was later identified as fifty-two-year-old Douglas Chandler. His broadcasts were
apparently pre-recorded on wax cylinders.

Constance Drexel, a former *Philadelphia Public Ledger* writer,
was given a brief try out by one of the American networks at
the start of the war. Shirer does not say which network, only
that she was dropped. Despite the fact that she was broadcasting for the Nazis, Shirer claims Drexel frequently pestered him
about a job with CBS.

Shirer also mentioned Fred Kaltenbach of Waterloo, Iowa,
whom he described as "not a bad radio speaker," and a fanat-
ical fascist who did not get along well with the Nazi authorities. Kaltenbach and Otto Koischwitz, as "Fred and Fritz," participated in   dramatized   conversations   over   the   German
shortwave station. Koischwitz, who was a former instructor at
New York City College, also broadcast as "Dr. Anders" and
"O.K.," the latter being his initials.

Jim and Johnny were the characters in a similar Nazi broadcast to North America. These two were supposed to be Cana-
dians, one of them a milkman. Jim would ask questions and
Johnny would provide the answers, which had the ring of the
Nazi propaganda line.

Another program featured Gertie, a switchboard operator for
the *Pittsburgh Tribune*, who had a boyfriend named Joe. He was
the paper's Berlin correspondent, and complained in letters to
Gertie—which she read aloud—that his Jewish editors kept

changing his copy and refused to let him tell the truth about Germany. The broadcast was called "Hot off the Wire," and Gertie was Gertrude Hohn. In addition to the letters from her boyfriend, the unlikely premise was put forward that phone calls to the *Pittsburgh Press* were monitored by the RRG and put over the air. There was no such paper in America when the series started, but ironically, a paper supported by the Pittsburgh black community began publishing under that masthead while "Hot off the Wire" was still on the air.

Only one French station beamed its signal to North America for propaganda purposes. Paris-Mondial had several Americans on its staff, but they were apparently not given much power in programming decisions, and less than a quarter of the French broadcasts heard in the United States were devoted to news and commentary.

The British Broadcasting Corporation had adopted a policy before war was declared, which was intended to keep its news factual. The policy statement was remarkably similar to the one put out jointly by the three American networks. A new agency had been formed, headed by former BBC chief Sir John Reith, and the British tried to use truth as their main weapon in a forceful presentation of their case to the world.

A special North American service was inaugurated on May 28, 1940. The announcer began it by saying: "Passionately I want my ideas—our ideas—of freedom and justice to survive."[30] Mutual, along with 138 independent stations, regularly carried material from the BBC service, and CBS and NBC also used it at times. The American network correspondents in Europe were also heard on BBC domestic and empire broadcasts. This was apparently in exchange for material on the BBC North American service, because the network correspondents individually were not compensated by the BBC. Because the BBC did not have the ban on recordings which CBS and NBC practiced, occasionally they heard themselves, either in England or on short wave reports beamed to Europe.[31]

There were even broadcasts which offered critiques of the propaganda. The BBC North American service and Australian radio both had programs which analyzed German and Italian propaganda.

In addition to the network shortwave monitoring facilities on

Long Island, two other listening centers existed which published studies of the foreign broadcasts beamed toward America. The Princeton Listening Center was the largest listening post in the United States, operating twelve hours daily. Its receivers were powerful—a Hammarland H.Q. 120 and a National N.C. 100. L. C. Gray reported that four transcribers worked at a time, listening to Dictaphone Telecord cylinders which could be shaved and reused.

The Princeton Listening Center grew out of a conversation between Professor John B. Whitton of Princeton University and Edward R. Murrow, CBS London correspondent, in the winter of 1938. It was set up as part of Princeton University's School of Public and International Affairs.[32]

Eleven men and women worked at the center, with competent transcribers in high demand. There were many instances of seemingly shocking news turning routine when the recording was checked. For instance, "many American consular officers are being shot down," was actually the more mundane "many consular offices are being shut down."

The listening center transcribed about sixty-five programs a day, and was funded by the Rockefeller Foundation. The opinion was that, after monitoring all kinds of broadcasts from Europe, Italy's reports before it entered the war were most reliable.

The second monitoring facility offering analysis of broadcasts from overseas was operated by B. E. Lucas, a columnist for the *Chicago Times*. He had started tuning in every day in January 1939 and started providing a day-by-day analysis October 10, 1939. A good part of his column was devoted to what his service picked up.

A brief piece in *The New Yorker* illustrated how all of the elements in foreign news coverage come together for CBS.[33] Paul White was talking to Murrow and Sevareid on the cue channel before a scheduled broadcast, the usual 6:45 P.M. roundup. The cue channel, which was used at both NBC and CBS, allowed the correspondents to hear staff members in New York. Sometimes the network air would be sent to them so they coud hear their introductions, and before and after broadcasts the channel would be used for making plans and other chit chat.

The anonymous author of the piece wrote:

We dropped in on [Paul White] the other evening at 6:30 P.M., fifteen minutes before program time. Mr. White told us that he is no longer thrilled by the idea, or execution, of transatlantic conversations. "For me," he said, "there's none of the fine careless rapture anymore." Perhaps his favorite conversation so far, he told us, was one with Edward R. Murrow, C.B.S.'s London man, to whose wife Mrs. White had written, unbeknowst to Mr. White, requesting a special kind of British yarn to use for the neck of an unfinished sweater she was knitting as a surpise Christmas present for her husband. "About your wife's yarn," said Murrow suddenly one evening, startling his boss. "What?" said White. "Can't get it," said Murrow. "My wife's been to five shops, and they all said they couldn't deliver any more till after the war."[34]

The night the man from the magazine was there the conversation was a little more serious. Murrow talked about the number of planes over the British coast that day, more than ever before. Sevareid was extremely upset about his script being cut by the censor, and Murrow said he would take some of the time which had been allotted to Sevareid. White talked with Murrow for a few minutes about taking a trip to Holland and about the broadcast schedule for the next week. Then, with air time a few minutes away, the chit-chat ceased.

In 1940, unless there was something which merited a special broadcast, the CBS correspondents were usually in the 6:45 P.M. roundup, as well as a new one which started that year and was heard in the East at 8 A.M.

The NBC schedule was similar, except that the NBC evening report was on an hour later than CBS's. In feeding the morning reports, however, there was sometimes some close scheduling, and Shirer might slip out of his chair in the RRG studios a few seconds before Jordan would start talking.

NOTES

1. Robert Metz, CBS: *Reflections in a Bloodshot Eye* (Chicago: Playboy Press, 1975), p. 99.

2. Edward Bliss, Jr., *In Search of Light: The Broadcasts of Edward R. Murrow* (New York: Knopf, 1967), p. 6.

3. Sevareid, *Not So Wild a Dream*, p. 113.

4. Jordan, *Beyond All Fronts*, p. 272.

5. Shirer, *Berlin Diary*, p. 257.

6. Ibid., pp. 256–57.

7. George N. Gordon and Irving A. Falk, *On the Spot Reporting: Radio Records History* (New York: J. Messner, 1967), p. 113.

8. Mary Marvin Breckinridge, interview with the author, May 10, 1981.

9. Ibid.

10. Ibid.

11. Janet Murrow, interview with the author, April 17, 1981.

12. Larry Lesueur, interview with the author, November 24, 1981.

13. Cecil B. Brown, interview with the author, January 30, 1981.

14. Ibid.

15. Betty Wason, interview with the author, June 5, 1981.

16. Ibid.

17. Ibid.

18. Ibid.

19. *Current Biography, 1943* (Detroit: Gale Research Co., 1943), p. 806.

20. Margaret Rupli Woodward, interview with the author, December 26, 1981.

21. Breckinridge, interview with the author, May 10, 1981.

22. Ibid.

23. Both Shirer and Flannery spell it *"Kerker."* Barnouw spells it *"Keirker."*

24. Harry W. Flannery, *Assignment to Berlin* (New York: Knopf, 1942), p. 29.

25. CBS Research Library, New York, no date.

26. Charles J. Rolo, *Radio Goes to War* (New York: Putnam, 1940), p. 122–23.

27. Paul Douglas, "Short Wave Listening," *Public Opinion Quarterly*, Vol. 5, June 1941.

28. Joyce was variously referred to as "Hee Haw" and "Haw Haw."

29. E. J. Kahn, Jr., "A Reporter at Large," *The New Yorker*, Vol. 16, No. 11, April 27, 1940, pp. 39–48.

30. Rolo, *Radio Goes to War*, p. 184.

31. Sevareid, for instance, was on a ship fleeing France in June 1940 when he heard Shirer's famous broadcast with Kerker from Compiègne. See Sevareid, *Not So Wild a Dream*, p. 159; and Shirer, *Berlin Diary*, p. 303.

32. L. C. Gray, "America's Ears," *Current History and Forum*, Vol. 52, No. 7, January 10, 1941, p. 12.

33. "Fine, Careless Rapture," *The New Yorker*, Vol. 15, No. 49, January 20, 1940, p. 17.

34. Ibid.

6 · Covering the Blitzkrieg

The networks continued to build their staffs through 1940, but the number of correspondents hired over the winter had more than doubled the European contingents from a year before. And as winter turned to spring, the need for the new recruits was evident.

Rupli had not done very many broadcasts while Breckinridge was in Berlin in January, February, and March. But starting April 7, 1940, she broadcast twice a week, almost always on weekends. Most of the reports were from five to seven minutes long, although on April 13 she produced an elaborate program from the Dutch defense perimeter. It was done with the aid of a Dutch AVRO broadcasting mobile truck which relayed a signal to the main studios at Hilversum. The broadcast featured soldiers singing and a scripted interview with a captain in the military engineers explaining how Rhine River water was being used to guard against a possible invasion. Although the Dutch censors stopped her from naming the officer or the place where the interview was done, the government was very much interested in Rupli telling Americans about preparations for a possible invasion.

Rupli's voice was not as cultured as Breckinridge's, and she was unmistakably American, whereas Breckinridge spoke with an upper-class accent which was vaguely English. Even on old metal records, Rupli's reports come across well. Rupli's husband at the time, David Woodward, feels that she never really hit her stride because of her infrequent broadcasting initially and then the shortness of her radio career. But he was very familiar with the work of Breckinridge and Schultz, and he has admiration for it. Schultz, he feels, was the superior reporter and was also very helpful to colleagues, especially if they were not in direct competition with her. While stationed in Amsterdam, he would frequently phone her for updates from Berlin and to swap the latest news from Holland.

Back in the Netherlands, Breckinridge knew that it was just a matter of time before an invasion. Patterson visited her twice in Holland, taking advantage of his diplomatic privileges to take a bushel of oysters back to the shellfish-loving Shirer on the return leg of the first trip. "The second time he couldn't bring the car across the border because the Germans had closed it. He had to take the train, and he noticed that the Dutch direction signs had been taken down."[1]

The couple tried to forget the war by renting a car over Whitsun and driving out into the country to see the tulips. They passed Dutch families on picnics and Patterson remarked that it was hard to understand how they could be so happy since the invasion was supposed to begin that day, May 5. Hitler had delayed the new grab for territory, putting it off on a day-by-day basis until May 10.

Breckinridge did nine broadcasts after she returned to Holland. Her final assignment involved an inspection of the Dutch battleship *Sumatra* on May 7. Breckinridge thinks the day-long voyage made her the only woman besides the Queen of the Netherlands to have been on a Dutch battleship at sea.

In the last day before the Nazi blitzkrieg, neither woman communicated the imminence of the attack. On May 8, Rupli reported that the government had issued an alert, but she also pointed out that there had been other alerts in the past, and that the government was saying this one was due to general international uncertainties and nothing specific to Holland.

Breckinridge left on the night of May 8, taking the last train to get through to Paris. Rupli stayed on, beginning her report on the morning of May 9: "I am glad to be able to report that all is quite calm and peaceful here tonight and tension has relaxed. . . . I feel quite sure that the group of soldiers that marches by my window tomorrow morning will be engaged in maneuvers and in nothing more serious."[2]

The soldiers the next day were busy defending their country, and bombs were dropping around the studio as Rupli tried to get a script approved for broadcast. Jordan wrote in *Beyond All Fronts*:

In Amsterdam, Margaret Rupli stood by for NBC while air-raid sirens were wailing, and enemy bombers were flying over the city.

Over the shortwave circuit connecting with New York she asked: "What do you want to know?"

"Everything! Just tell us what you see!" replied the program director.

That moment the hisses and screech of falling bombs were heard. "I've got to run!" said Miss Rupli.

"Oh, don't leave! Let's hear the bombs!" was the program director's reply.[3]

Schechter says the program director in Jordan's account was really himself, the news director. But the rest of the account is factual, says Rupli. She had been at the Hilversum studios for her reassuring report on the night before the invasion and then was returning to Amsterdam early in the morning when the invasion started. She was never able to clear a report through the Dutch censors before fleeing.

Because her husband was a British citizen and likely to be taken into custody if the Nazis were in charge in Holland, Rupli decided to leave, even though NBC offered her a staff position if she would stay. "David said he wouldn't leave without me, and that decided it."[4] They escaped on a vessel pressed into service.

It was a little Bitish coal barge that had been overlooked. They came up to the British Embassy in The Hague and said "Have you got anybody you want to put on?" It was a very motley crew: mixed marriages, British aviators who had been shot down for violating Dutch neutrality and now were freed, and the Sadler's Wells Ballet. There was straw in the hold and I remember I had David on one side of me. He had picked up a bottle of whiskey, and I had picked up toothbrushes and things like that. I remember it was the only time I got deliberately tight because I thought "If I'm going down in the North Sea, there's no point of being sober." I had a banana, a piece of chocolate, and about a cup full of whiskey, and then I snuggled up and went to sleep. And when I woke up in the morning, there was a shaft of light coming down into the hold, and I clambered up the ladder, and here were the Sadler's Wells people doing exercises on this narrow little walkway. And overhead was this absolutely gorgeous British plane circling around.[5]

The captain of the little ship had abandoned his plan to keep close to the coast and had plunged out into the Channel. The lowly coal barge had arrived in Harwich at the same time the Queen of the Netherlands had arrived on a British destroyer. The aerial escort was for the royalty.

Rupli had her own set of jewels, however: "I was laden with diamonds because a Jewish refugee woman had sent me everything she had to take to her sister. I had a diamond watch, I had my own diamond ring, and I had two or three diamond rings on my other hand. I just wore them in, and nobody said a word."[6]

The Woodwards went straight to London. Rupli had prepared a broadcast on the fall of Holland and was ready to give it when they arrived in London. But by then interest had shifted to Belgium, and she was put on the air only because a scheduled report from Brussels could not be aired. Rupli was delighted that Murrow, who was monitoring the NBC feed, heard her report and phoned to compliment his one-time student.

Later that month, Rupli returned to America on the *President Roosevelt* and did a final broadcast for NBC as the ship came into New York. She wanted to continue broadcasting in America, but she was offered only one broadcast a week on NBC in midmorning and did not feel that was worthwhile. Instead, she went back to work for the Department of Labor.

CBS was not left without coverage in Holland when Breckinridge went to Paris. Edwin Hartrich was there to pick up for her, but only by chance. Hartrich was then twenty-eight and had been with CBS for just a few months. A newspaper man who had attended Notre Dame and Northwestern, he had been a Washington correspondent before heading overseas in the midthirties. First he worked for *Time* magazine in London. Then he landed a job on the *Paris Herald-Tribune*. Sevareid was one of his colleagues, but it was another reporter on the paper who got Hartrich started with CBS. Walter Kerr had gone up to cover the war in Finland, and when William L. White left his CBS post there, Kerr tipped off Hartrich about the job opportunity. He filled in for a while and then went back to Paris.

Hartrich, like a lot of other print people, had strung for NBC at the start of the war. CBS wanted a reporter in Denmark, and Hartrich had gone down to Paris in May to pick up some clothes and other belongings before heading for Copenhagen. In order to get to Denmark, Hartrich needed visas. In Brussels, there were problems getting to Amsterdam. Once that difficulty was resolved, he could not get approval to travel to Denmark, possibly because the Nazis did not want a reporter to see preparations for the invasion.

Shirer, who had good information that something was going to happen in Holland, sent a telegram to New York asking that Hartrich be held up in Amsterdam. So Hartrich spent the night of May 9 in the Carlton.

We were awakened about four or five in the morning by the sound of gunfire, and the hotel we were staying in was about eight stories, so we went up on the roof to see. We could see the smoke and hear shooting, explosions. From the information we could gather, it looked like a German attack on The Hague, the capital. So I and a couple of guys—Norman Alley of the newsreel people and Ike Conger of the *New York Herald Tribune*—got a car and drove down. And just outside The Hague we ran into a shooting match. We had to dive out of the car and into the bushes. The Germans were in the field, and the Dutch were fighting them, and we got the hell out of there.[7]

Hartrich was able to get one report out, and then he started filing copy to New York when broadcasting was banned. In a few days he went to Berlin, where he assisted Shirer for the next six months. In November he went home for a vacation, and the Germans refused him a visa to return, so he went to cover the Far East.

Another new voice was added to CBS in May 1940. Winston Burdette got his job as a direct result of the network's displeasure over Betty Wason's delivery. Wason had continued re-

porting from Scandinavia but received a request in May to cease
her reporting and find a man to broadcast. "I received a call
saying my voice wasn't coming through, that it was too young
and feminine for war news and that the public was objecting to
it."[8]

It is true that Wason's broadcasting style was not as assured
as Rupli's or as low-pitched as Breckinridge's. She sometimes
ran out of breath and stumbled more often. But the voice defi-
nitely came through, and her writing was very good. Wason is
convinced she was a victim of male prejudice.

There were indications that women were not favored by the
public. A study of attitudes toward radio in America in the mid–
1930s had found that the majority of Americans wanted to get
their news from a man, and that women were less objectionable on the air if they were reading a commercial or some form
of literature.[9] The feelings of the network executives seemed to
mirror those of the public. Harry W. Flannery, who joined CBS
in late 1940 as Shirer's replacement in Berlin, found that Columbia did not favor women on the air—especially from foreign points. The reason, he felt, was that male listeners preferred male voices and did not have confidence in what was
reported by women, even though the reporting was equally
good.[10]

Wason went to Winston Burdette, who was working for
Transradio. "I helped coach him on his first broadcast, and
taught him how to write for radio, which I had learned the hard
way."[11] Burdette had been born in Buffalo, New York, on December 12, 1913. He had graduated magna cum laude at Harvard and had done graduate work at Columbia. He started
working for the *Brooklyn Eagle* as a movie and book reviewer
and then worked as a reporter for *The Sound Track* and *The Trend*.
In 1940, he went to Europe, working for minimal money as a
Transradio reporter.

Wason had told Transradio that she could not work for them
while working for CBS. But Burdette kept his Transradio job
while stringing for CBS, and so Wason had to move on to new
territory. She went to the Balkans, the newest hot spot, but
Burdette soon followed. Wason tried Turkey, filing a few stories for Transradio from there. When it was evident that fight-

ing would flare up in Greece, she went to Athens and started reporting for CBS again. The reaction to her voice was the same as before, however, and once again she was asked to find a man to broadcast. "I found a man in the American Embassy who served as my voice, saying 'I'm Phil Brown speaking for Betty Wason.' "[12] Brown was not his real name, and it is one of a number of instances where reporters did not use their correct names when reporting for the networks from Europe.

Wason broadcast only once more for herself from Greece prior to Nazi occupation. She had been to the front lines and wanted people back in America to know it—whether her voice was judged frail or not. She continued to run the CBS bureau in Athens, living with the disappointment of not being able to speak for herself. "I knew I was an excellent reporter, and yet they said my voice did not come across. Well, I have done so much broadcasting since then that I know my voice was good, and it was just the objection to a woman's voice giving news."[13]

After the Nazis occupied Athens, Wason and several other American reporters were not allowed to leave. For almost two months they were stranded, until the Germans transported them to Berlin. After learning that CBS had no further need of her services, Wason returned to America.

NOTES

1. Breckinridge, interview with the author, May 10, 1981.
2. Margaret Rupli Woodward script, May 9, 1940, held by Woodward.
3. Jordan, *Beyond All Fronts*, pp. 278–79.
4. Woodward interview, December 26, 1981.
5. Ibid.
6. Ibid.
7. Edwin Hartrich, interview with the author, July 17, 1981.
8. Wason, interview with the author, June 5, 1981.
9. Hadley Cantril and Gordon W. Allport, *The Psychology of Radio* (New York: Harper, 1935), p. 127.
10. Flannery, *Assignment to Berlin*, p. 108.
11. Wason, interview with the author, June 5, 1981.
12. Wason, interview with the author, December 26, 1981.
13. Ibid.

7 · The Fall of France

The Paris and Berlin network men had been watching the Nazi march through Scandinavia and expected the Low Countries to be next. Sevareid had gone to see how Holland was preparing for the invasion which seemed sure to come, and he found few fortifications, a number of soldiers AWOL from their assignments, and strict censorship. A cabinet member read his script and warned that the slightest deviation from it would result in Sevareid being cut off the air.

The American consul in Amsterdam, however, seemed little concerned with the possibility of war in Holland. When asked for some information about the Netherlands, he gave Sevareid a press release on tulips and then seemed genuinely amazed that a radio man would want to talk about war preparations and not flowers.

The night before the invasion, Shirer had been able to hint broadly in his broadcast from Berlin that the Nazis were moving toward the Low Countries. Jordan was probably in the United States, having picked a rather poor time for a conference with NBC officials.

In broadcasting details of the invasion the next day, Shirer was not allowed to call the sweep an invasion, at least not in the lead of his script. He fought briefly, but since he had used the word "invasion" three times further down in his script, Shirer compromised on the use of it in the first sentence. Actually, burying the lead in the end of the story was a common trick for foreign correspondents. In the case of print men, they relied on a sharp desk editor to notice where the meat of the story was and restore it to the lead.

Sevareid was also caught away from his bureau when the Nazis attacked the Low Countries. The Sevareids had become parents of twin boys on April 25, with William L. White coming down from Scandinavia to fill in for a few days. Even though Lois Sevareid was still not able to walk and was in a hospital, Eric left for Algeria on May 9 to line up correspondents in case Italy moved in that direction. He got as far as the small town of Valence, not far from Lyons, and awoke the next morning to find that the Nazis had struck. Breckinridge was there to assist Grandin, of course, but Sevareid knew he had to get back.

He rescued his wife from the hospital, which was rapidly losing both patients and staff in the flight from Paris. After finding a place in the French countryside for them, he went north to cover the fighting. At the Belgium border he witnessed a dogfight between two British fighters and a single German plane and rushed to the crater made when the Nazi craft crashed.

Deciding that a larger picture of the battles could be obtained by returning to Paris, Sevareid got on a long train filled with refugees from the north. What was usually a four-hour trip took eighteen hours. Sevareid stood through most of it, a trip he swore to remember forever. Two other reporters were on the train with him, Kenneth Downs of INS and Ralph Heinzen, and as they continued south, they also sensed they were going west. Long stretches where they did not move at all were made memorable by the crying of children on the mile-long train. Knowing where the French defense lines were, the reporters watched the artillery fire in the distance and timed the sound of bursts to confirm what they had suspected. The Germans had breached the French defense.

The three men were in journalistic agony. They had a scoop and no way to report it. Matters were only made worse when they arrived in Paris hours later and found the French censors would not let them tell the news to America.

Sevareid then resorted to a code system which he had set up for just such an instance. He had sent White a list with an innocuous phrase for each of several possible events, including the invasion of France. His message got through to New York, but the telegram sat on a newsroom desk for several hours until someone figured out what it was. News of the breach was

broadcast, attributed only to "a usually well-informed source."
It was the last time Sevareid used such a code.

The British Expeditionary Force in the war zone was pushed
back to Dunkirk, and its evacuation was begun on May 26, with
a new prime minister, Winston Churchill, leading his country-
men in hoping for a miracle which would save them. It came
in the form of hundreds of little boats which helped larger ones
save 200,000 British and 139,000 French and Belgian soldiers.

Belgium surrendered May 28, but the Dunkirk evacuation was
not completed until June 4, 1940. Part of the success of Dunkirk
was due to Nazi greed for Paris, for on June 3 the bombing of
that city began. Shirer got word of the bombing plans May 30.
He had been alternating between following the blitzkrieg with
a group of nine reporters, guided by German officials, and going
back to Berlin to report.

Bate and Murrow had been reporting the evacuation from the
British side, making frequent trips to the coastal airfields and
harbors to interview men as they returned from rescue. Then
they drove back to London to broadcast. The drive was some-
what hazardous because the British had removed all of the road
signs.

Sevareid had sent his wife and babies home on a liner that
sailed from Genoa. Tess Shirer and daughter Eileen were trying
to leave from Genoa on a ship for the United States but could
not make connections and finally went back to Geneva. Sevareid also lost his partner in Paris, Tom Grandin.

Grandin had gotten married in February after a whirlwind
romance with a Yugoslav shortwave broadcaster, Natalia Parligras. They had met while Grandin was there to cover some
meetings for CBS. Parligras was a specialist in Rumania and
broadcast programs for the government agency during the evening. Grandin apparently saw her first as he was preparing an
early morning feed on a conference of Balkan diplomats.

They got engaged one day and married the next after the
posting of the banns was waived. She did not speak English
and translated the Serbian vows into French. Interestingly, on
the official marriage forms, both claimed it was their first marriage. Grandin had actually been divorced several years earlier
in America.

The Sevareids and Grandins had shared an apartment in Paris which doubled as the bureau office. In early June, Grandin went with his wife to Bordeaux, in hopes of getting her on an America-bound ship. Mrs. Grandin was probably pregnant, and that may have affected his decision to join her, because Sevareid got a telegram from the port city saying that Grandin had decided to join his wife and sail for America. "I was left there with two newborn babies of my own. I got Edmund Taylor of the *Chicago Tribune*, a very fine writer and an old hand around Paris, to come and help me, and we were together for the collapse of Paris, our trip to Bordeaux, and our own exodus."[1]

Both NBC and CBS received reinforcements from women reporters. Helen Hiett joined the NBC bureau in mid-May. She had first come to Europe in 1934, the day after she graduated from the University of Chicago. Hiett had taken her political science degree in three years, and was given a scholarship to study at the League of Nations in Geneva. The daughter of the Superintendent of Schools in Pekin, Illinois, Hiett had been something of a protégée of F. F. McNaughton, editor of the *Pekin Daily Times*.

She arrived in Geneva after taking a steamer from New York to Southampton, and then on to Le Havre. Trains took her to Paris and then to Geneva. Hiett applied for a press pass almost immediately upon arriving in Geneva, probably so she could get material for articles to be sent back to Pekin. That summer she studied public opinion concerning the league, and when her scholarship ran out, she got a job as a secretary and souvenir seller at the Geneva Research Center. The salary was sixty-six dollars a month.

Because of illness and resignations, Hiett suddenly found herself editing the monthly research center newsletter. She also wrote articles for the *Daily Times* back home, and took courses at the Graduate Institute of International Studies. Hiett left Geneva in the summer of 1936 to see for herself how the Italians were undermining the League of Nations sanctions, and then she went home to America in 1937. She returned to begin a Ph.D. program at the London School of Economics on a scholarship from the Federation of American Women's Clubs Overseas.

Before starting classes, Hiett spent several weeks living in a German girls' work camp, and she came away with a deep dislike of the human manipulation she saw there. When the war started, she abandoned her dissertation and moved to France. Frustrated that the French were not using radio to develop patriotism at home or garner support from America, she tried to convince Radio Mondial authorities in Paris to let her broadcast to the United States. She sent memos containing ideas for broadcasts to the director of overseas operations for the radio agency, but with no success.

Finally, one day in October 1939, a telegram arrived at her apartment requesting that Hiett appear at the broadcast agency studios on the outskirts of Paris at two o'clock in the morning. She arrived after an ordeal in getting there on a dark, rainy night. There was a blackout, and she had fallen down and hurt herself. Once at the studio, she was disappointed to learn that her assignment was to read a poorly translated version of a short story by Victor Hugo.

By January 1940, Hiett had decided that Americans might be moved by a newsletter which gave a real idea of what was happening in the war. Called *Paris Letter*, it offered accounts of life in Paris and letters from soldiers at the front. Hiett was also able to write about some things which the regular foreign correspondents could not. For instance, during Easter Week, she was able to get a good look at the front, which was off limits to most journalists. Hiett did so because she was invited for the holiday by a family living near Metz, and she toured the French defenses as a guest.

The newsletter met with some success, and capitalizing on that and a desire to spread the word in person, Hiett took a berth on the *Rex* in early April and sailed from Genoa to America, where she embarked on a lecture tour. Her last talk was on May 10 in Rochester, New York. A speech to an advertising club was carried on local radio, except for the last part, which was cut due to other program commitments. Hiett had learned of the invasion of the Low Countries just before she started speaking and apparently gave an impassioned talk. The termination of the broadcast upset a number of listeners, who called to complain.

Hiett had planned to return to Illinois for a vacation after her tour, but at the suggestion of one of the people who heard her speech, she flew instead to New York and made appointments with the CBS and NBC news directors. Although Schechter does not remember things happening in quite this order, the account Hiett gives tells of an appointment with Schechter on May 13. Jordan was in New York to talk with Schechter about plans for future European coverage, and both men interviewed Hiett. Jordan, who spoke eight languages, was impressed that Hiett spoke four.

The two men apparently asked Hiett if she would be able to work in Berlin, but she forthrightly said she would not be able to tolerate close contact with the Nazis. She wanted to go to Paris, but NBC had Paul Archinard there, and the interview ended with Hiett being told that they would get back to her.

The CBS interview went even worse, apparently, for Hiett makes no further mention of it.[2] She waited a week for word from NBC and was giving up hope when she made a visit to Schechter's office on Saturday, May 18. Hiett had already bought a ticket to Pekin, and was going to give the NBC people her Illinois address.

But Schechter, who was in on that Saturday, had apparently decided to hire Hiett as an assistant to Archinard, who was carrying a heavy load in Paris. Visas had been obtained for Portugal and Spain, and Hiett would be able to take over Jordan's reservation on a Clippership flight to Europe. But NBC had been unable to secure a French visa. In fact, they had been told that it would take over a month to obtain one.

Hiett writes that she took her passport and rushed across the street from the NBC building to the French Consulate. It was just a few minutes before closing time, but an official there knew about the *Paris Letter*, and Hiett got the visa. She left the next day and was in Paris by May 21, 1940. "I had to start broadcasting at once to take some of the strain off Paul Archinard, who had been doing five and six shows a day with little chance for sleep in between."[3]

Unlike most of the other radio correspondents, Hiett had apparently not undergone a voice test before being hired. But she

quickly got some feedback on what she had put in her scripts
in her early broadcasts from Paris. Describing the condition of
refugees at an aid station where she did volunteer work, Hiett
mentioned that some children had such severe blisters on their
feet that skin came off when their shoes and socks were removed. She recalled that a chiding voice came back over the
cue channel from New York after the broadcast. "That was bad
judgement. Don't forget, some Americans will be at the breakfast table when they are listening to you. We don't want any
more of that kind of stuff. And you are never to mention the
word 'blood'."[4]
   Like broadcast foreign correspondents before her, Hiett found
the French censorship frustrating.

In contrast to press correspondents whose work was done when they
had filed dispatches with the censor, those of us reporting news by
radio had the most nerve-racking part of the job still ahead of us once
we had delivered our scripts to the censors in the Hotel Continental.
Then there was the interminable waiting until the script was returned;
the probability that, with the censor's deletions, it would no longer
make sense to the listening audience; the impossibility of finding a
conveyance to get across Paris in the blackout to the studio; and the
frequent discouragement of reaching the microphone as New York
stopped calling "Come in Paris," thus, too late to go on the air, the
day's work done in vain.[5]

   The beginning of Hiett's broadcast career was, of course, at
the end of free France. Paris was bombed on Monday, June 3.
As Archinard was talking to New York, the NBC office was hit.
Hiett, who had been at the government broadcasting center
when the raid began, emerged from a bomb shelter there and
made for the apartment at 15 Rue Poussin which doubled as
the NBC office. Unable to get the full distance by taxi, she walked
the last way past rubble to find Archinard and a secretary digging through the wrecked office. Just then the phone started
ringing and it was New York again, urging Archinard to get
out in the streets with a microphone the next time the bombing
started. The network officials wanted to put the sounds of war
on the air.

Breckinridge had also been pressed into service as soon as she arrived in Paris from Amsterdam. On May 10, she reported on the state of tension in Holland at the time she departed. On the twelfth, she received the bad news from someone at the American Embassy that her marriage meant an end to her broadcasting for CBS. She would not be allowed to report as long as she was married to a diplomat representing the United States.

The next day she obtained a gas mask and interviewed refugees who arrived at the Gare du Nord from the Low Countries. On May 17, Breckinridge reported on a civil defense plan for Paris, and in great contrast to the destruction about which she was reporting, bought some bridal accessories. On May 18, she did two broadcasts, and over the next two weeks, five more.

Breckinridge's last broadcast for CBS was on June 5, 1940. It was a report on a village south of Paris which was already seeing a stream of refugees pass through as Paris wobbled toward collapse. Breckinridge decided to leave too after she learned that the French government was abandoning the city. There was little chance for further broadcasts from Paris, and she felt that if you could not get your story out, there was no sense in staying. And she also felt she had given CBS plenty of notice that she was leaving for Berlin to be married.

On June 8, 1940, at 8:25 P.M., Breckinridge left Paris for the Gare de Lyon, heading for Italy. Because passengers had to have an exit permit and visa, there were few last minute additions to the passenger list, and the train was not unusually crowded. After a delay in Genoa, she arrived in Berlin on June 16. She married Jefferson Patterson on June 20 and had a three-day honeymoon near Munich before turning to the grim task of accompanying her husband as he inspected prisoner-of-war camps.

Sevareid, too, was wrestling with the ethical dilemma of what should be reported. As Paris was under attack, he continued to broadcast but wondered what to say.

For what is a journalist's duty? Suppose he was clear in the knowledge that France was going down, that the game was up. Had he the right to say this to the world and thus to the French themselves, to join, in effect, the Nazi propagandists, so long as the miracle of military accident might still come about? It was the first time I had been confronted with the basic problem of reconciling the conflict of professional duty to a universal cause. "The truth is its own justification," I had always been taught and always believed. But was it? Was this always so, at all times? I was unable to decide.[6]

CBS had given Sevareid orders to leave Paris if the French government did. His last broadcast from Paris was on June 10, 1940, the same day Italy attacked France and declared war on Britain as well. The French broadcasting agency kept the shortwave station open for his last piece, which almost did not get on the air because a bureaucratic form had not been filled out.

In that final broadcast, Sevareid stated that if American listeners were to hear a radio voice from Paris again, "It would be under jurisdiction other than French."[7] Worried as usual about censorship, he found that this time his message would be transmitted as written. That broadcast was the means by which most Americans found out that Paris had fallen. The Germans made much of his report, translating parts of it for broadcast over the RRG. Shirer heard it and knew he would soon see Paris, but a Paris in Nazi hands. It would be "the saddest assignment of my life."[8]

As Sevareid joined the thousands fleeing south from Paris, he found a shortwave station operating in central France, and linked to it by phone lines, he and Taylor broadcast from Tours. In order for broadcasts to be carried by CBS, however, he had to get word to them about which frequency to monitor. A friendly newspaperman with a Press Wireless machine got the message through.

Lesueur linked up with Sevareid in Tours, but only briefly. Because he was attached to the British Advanced Air Striking Force, and because he was under British orders, Lesueur was supposed to be on a troop train before Paris fell. But he had made some friends while in France, Americans Persis Woodward and her daughter Ruth. They were in Paris, and Lesueur wanted to warn them that the city would.fall. So he then was to go with the British Headquarters as it moved south. Taking the two women, he traveled in a car to Troyes and put them up in a hotel. Traveling during the night, he then got to Tours, where Sevareid told him not to worry, that CBS was being taken care of. The next stop for Lesueur was Blois, and then Nantes, where he was to catch a British troop carrier in the port of St.-Nazaire. But the gangplank was pulled up as he was trying to get on board; the ship was full. It was a piece of fate like so many others in those days of the war. As the ship was leaving the harbor, a Stuka dive-bomber came over and dropped a bomb down the ship's smokestack. The engine room exploded, and several thousand people on board were killed. Lesueur did not see the carnage. By then he was in a truck carrying British personnel north to Brest. Another troop ship was waiting there, and it took Lesueur safely from France on June 17.

Sevareid kept working. When the French government fled again, this time to Bordeaux, Taylor and Sevareid kept broadcasting using the same transmitter. In New York, the CBS shortwave listening staff had been tuned into the Bordeaux-Lafayette transmitter for forty-eight hours, trying to get any news about France. They were startled to hear a voice saying "Calling CBS listening station in New York, calling CBS listening station in New York."[9]

Not only would they be getting news from their own correspondent, but the cylinders normally used to record foreign broadcasts for transcription were soon used to take copy from newspaper and wire service reporters in Bordeaux. The copy was then relayed to the reporters' New York offices. Sevareid scored a number of scoops. "Eighty percent resulted from pure chance; the other 20 percent from correct thinking (or guessing), legwork, and intimate knowledge of communication facilities."[10]

One of his broadcasts detailed the ascendancy of Marshal Pétain to premier. Sevareid was so concerned about getting the news to America that he forgot to get the script approved by the censors, who had also moved south with the government. Then he noticed that there was no minister of information on the list of new cabinet members he had been given. And no one challenged him when he began to broadcast. The studio the correspondents were using was on the outskirts of Bordeaux, and Sevareid arrived there to find Archinard had already broadcast the news on the change of government. But he also learned that Archinard was reporting the Pétain government was determined to continue the fight. Sevareid was convinced it would sue for peace, and apparently having solved his dilemma, he spoke without a script or censorship and conveyed that conviction to CBS listeners. Two days later, he and the Taylors (she had accompanied them south) were on board a Belgian ship crowded with refugees and bound for England. He did not know if he had a job or if any of his broadcasts had gotten through.

Archinard was in Bordeaux after a ride with his NBC staff which roughly paralleled Sevareid's. They had departed on Monday, June 10, and had done day and night broadcasts from Tours for the three days the French government tarried there. On June 14, they moved to Bordeaux. Hiett had taken along a backpack and a bedroll and had been using them, sleeping in fields at times. She used a coal bin as her writing headquarters in Tours. Now in Bordeaux, the news was the transition to the Vichy government. Along with the CBS men, Waverly Root was there for Mutual.

But when Sevareid and Taylor left, Hiett and Archinard stayed on. She had not had a bath in ten days. He was concerned about the safety of his family and left to try and find them in the French countryside.[11] On June 19, Hiett reported the names of the men selected to negotiate the French surrender. And until June 22, she continued to report over the only remaining transmitter. With the Nazi takeover of France that day, she could broadcast no more.

Hiett had run into some old friends from the *Paris Letter* during her last days in Bordeaux, and they decided to try to reach a house in southern France where they would be safe. Driving a car given to one of the young women in the melee which preceded the departure of ships from Bordeaux, the carload of women sped south. At times, they shared the road with Nazi troop carriers. But they did reach the house, whereupon Hiett decided to try to get to Switzerland, where she could broadcast the rest of her story on the fall of France.

Hiett reached Geneva on the Fourth of July. After doing her broadcast, she conferred with network officials about her next assignment. Spain was one possibility, the Balkans another. Sweden was a third. Hiett chose Spain, a selection which resulted in a good deal of frustration and little broadcasting.

Sweden would not have been much better, but the Balkans were to become the next hot spot for broadcast foreign correspondents.

Hiett went to Madrid, where she found Spanish censorship to be extreme and interest from New York in Spanish affairs to be modest. She did manage to score a scoop on the bombing of Gibraltar in late 1940 but was able to give her eyewitness account only by leaving the island, which had no powerful shortwave transmitter. She went back to Madrid to broadcast her exclusive but was initially blocked by the government. Then she was thwarted twice because sunspots made transmissions fuzzy. Finally she got her story out. But from it, she became the first woman to win the National Headliners Club award.

When Spanish authorities made broadcasting from that country a near impossibility for her, Hiett returned to the United States and became a daily news commentator for NBC. She left that post eighteen months later to become a guest lecturer at Stephens College in Missouri and then returned to Europe as a print correspondent until the end of the war.

With the Paris-based correspondents gone, any reporting from France was up to the Americans accredited by the Nazis. Shirer left Berlin for Paris on June 15. Six miles out of Berlin his car broke down. The next day he continued on, going through Liège, Namur, and Maubeuge, and arriving in Paris on June 17. He was one of twelve foreign correspondents accredited to the occupying German Army.

It was a beautiful day, but the streets were deserted. Shirer stopped briefly at the building where he had worked fifteen years before and continued a walking tour of his old haunts—now haunted.

On June 19, Shirer learned through a Nazi mistake that Hitler planned to force the defeated French to sign an armistice at Compiègne. The site was important, for at 5 A.M. on November 11, 1918, the German surrender had been formalized in a railway car in the Compiègne forest about forty-five miles north of Paris. Marshal Foch's compartment, where the signings had taken place, had been preserved in a museum there. Place cards showed where the representatives of the victors and the vanquished had been sitting or standing.

The Germans in charge of broadcasting from Paris rushed

Shirer to Compiègne, perhaps thinking the signing was going to take place almost immediately. He arrived to find the wall of the museum being destroyed so that the railway car could be removed and placed in the exact spot where it had stood in 1918. Arrangements were made for a broadcast of the signing— whenever it might occur—and then Shirer was taken back to Paris.

Two days later the German terms were delivered to the French, with Hitler sitting where Foch had twenty-one years before. Shirer and Kerker did a joint broadcast carried by both networks in America and the BBC as well. In a strange coincidence, a radio was turned on in the cabin where Sevareid was sitting on board the Belgian ship carrying him to Britain, and he heard Shirer and Kerker describing the scene as they stood on the perimeter of the clearing in the forest.

Hitler stayed a half hour only, his reversal of the past symbolically performed. The meetings continued without him, and the armistice was signed the next day, June 22, 1940. Again Kerker and Shirer did a joint broadcast, Shirer obtaining details by snooping around in the forest. The Germans had hidden microphones in the train car and were probably recording the whole ceremony.[12]

NOTES

1. Sevareid, interview with the author, November 6, 1980.
2. CBS news officials tended to make no commitments in America; they let the European staff do the hiring, principally, Murrow. It is unlikely Hiett got anything more than the introductory encouragement that Wason got.
3. Helen Hiett, No Matter Where (New York: Dutton, 1944), p. 206.
4. Ibid., p. 207.
5. Ibid., p. 208.
6. Sevareid, Not So Wild a Dream, p. 143.
7. Ibid., p. 146.
8. Shirer, Berlin Diary, p. 403.
9. Gray, "America's Ears," p. 12.
10. Sevareid, Not So Wild a Dream, p. 152.
11. Hiett, No Matter Where, p. 212.
12. Shirer, Berlin Diary, p. 427.

8 · Battle of Britain

Britain stood alone. But the fall of France actually helped the network bureaus in London beef up for what was coming. Sevareid's ship, having gone well to the west before turning north, touched British shore in Belfast, then crossed over to Liverpool. There was some delay in immigration, for the trio had been listed as apprentice seamen on the captain's crew roster, a situation given little credence by British immigration officials. Sevareid was allowed to go ashore to phone Murrow, and soon Sevareid and the Taylors were on a train to London. Murrow had told Sevareid on the phone that their broadcasts from France had indeed been received. "You and Taylor have pulled off one of the greatest broadcasting feats there ever was. Come on to London—there's work to be done here."[1]

It was July 1, 1940. Lesueur had returned about a week earlier. For the rest of the summer, they would make what Murrow said about the CBS work in France apply to that in Britain.

NBC was also beefing up. John MacVane was hired to assist Fred Bate. Jordan was back from America and had been to occupied Paris and also some of Belgium. Archinard, who had not been able to find his family, finally went back to Vichy France and became one of the few reporters to cover it from inside French borders.

MacVane had left Paris June 10 on the orders of International News Service bosses in New York. Kenneth Downs, who was the INS bureau chief in Paris, and John and Lucy MacVane and several other INS people had gone to Tours and then Bordeaux as the Taylors and Sevareid had. They also got on a boat to England and from there were going to catch a ship or plane back to the United States.

While in England, explains MacVane, they talked to some of the London correspondents. "Fred Bate saw Ken Downs, he was an old friend, and said, 'Ken, would you join NBC, and cover the invasion of England by the Germans?' And Ken said, 'Why sure, Fred, I would. I want $190 a week.' And Fred said, 'Oh, Ken you know NBC can't pay any price like that. Do you know anybody who'd do it cheaper?' And Ken said 'You might try John MacVane, he's not doing anything, he's just going home with me.' So Fred said, 'John, would you take this job for $125 a week?' I said, 'I certainly will, Fred.' "[2] It was twice what MacVane had been making with INS. With the first week's pay, he went out and bought his wife a silver fox fur. He felt rich.

The twenty-eight-year-old Macvane had been getting sixty-five dollars a week with INS. He was following Bate around, learning the ropes. That included the policy on unbiased reporting. "Fred Bate and Ed Murrow laid down this rule to us. They decided themselves that they would not sensationalize the war; the war was sensational enough by itself. Just play it straight, absolutely factual, no excitement or anything like that. Don't try to whip anyone's feelings up. Just tell it like it is, calmly and straightforward. It was sometimes difficult. Sometimes you felt so strongly one way or another, that it was hard to do it, but we did, we tried."[3]

Sevareid, thirty years after it happened, described England during the summer of 1940 as a broadcaster's Camelot.

Churchill speaking to the whole world. J. B. Priestley speaking to his own people. Ed Murrrow speaking to America each night, the timbre of his powerful, steady voice reflecting the spirit of England and persuading millions of Americans that the cause was not lost even when it seemed beyond saving. . . . It was in those months . . . that radio came into its own. The men, the instrument, the moment were perfectly met. It has never been the same since, by radio or television. I doubt that television, no matter the circumstances, can match that performance by radio. Because the pictures reduce all to literalness; they cannot show an idea or a value; they block out the imagination of the listener; they have no eloquence.[4]

In the six weeks between the fall of France and the first mass bombing of England, the British had transformed their island into a fortress. The network correspondents made frequent trips to examine the defenses. Starting August 5, the German attack began in earnest. Again, the reporters for the networks went to see the action. Bate and Murrow were driving together near the Portland Navy Base when it was bombed, and they stopped to watch the British ground response to the German planes overhead.

As the bombing intensified in the Battle of Britain, MacVane wanted to test his wings in describing the dogfights which were taking place. He went to Croydon, where the airfield had been under attack, and, along with BBC newsman Edward Ward, used one of the BBC's recording machines. "We recorded something to have it ready so that when the big bombing began we could concentrate on that. I was pretty dismayed at hearing myself, my quavering voice. And hearing Eddie Ward, now Lord Bangor, his voice was so good and steady and mine (so shaky), but I got it under control after that, after hearing myself."[5]

MacVane had not intended to use the recording for a broadcast, but on several occasions the CBS correspondents did violate the network ban on recordings. About the same time MacVane was practicing with the BBC recorder, Sevareid was experimenting with one. "I went down to Dover and recorded some bombing and dogfights and whatnot that we put over, but the BBC engineers forgot to put the gain up and it sounded just ridiculous. It didn't work well. But then I remember when Ed was back here [in the United States, probably in late 1941] we went to the Pentagon and looked at the wire machines they had. He had this in his mind all the time."[6]

In an effort to convince the British censors that he was capable of broadcasting live during a bombing attack without giving away British military secrets, Murrow did a series of audition recordings using BBC equipment. "I had to stand on a rooftop for six nights in succession and make a record each night and submit it to the Ministry of Information in order to persuade the censors that I could ad lib without violating security. And I did it for six nights and the records were lost somewhere in the Ministry of Information, so then I had to do it for another six nights before they would finally give me permission after listening to the second take of six, to stand on a roof-top."[7]

There are indications that a small number of Murrow's later rooftop reports might have been recorded in a similar fashion and broadcast as if they were being done live.[8] Shirer concurs. "We never said so publicly, but Ed and I, and maybe some of the others, I don't know, cheated occasionally. You couldn't cover a war with a telephone wire. We couldn't get there fast enough. Or Ed couldn't cover the bombing because he'd go up there on the evening news and that would be the three minutes that the Germans wouldn't be overhead to give him any sound. So he did some recording there and I did some recording up at the front."[9]

Shirer's recordings, and he says there were few of them, were done with German RRG equipment. He had received an offer to use their recorders just a few days after the fighting had started in 1939. "The Germans say they will let me do radio recordings at the front, but American networks won't permit the broadcasting of my recordings—a pity because it is the only way radio can really cover the war from the front. I think we're throwing away a tremendous opportunity, though God knows I have no desire to die a hero's death at the front."[10]

MacVane believes that even the BBC reporters had an advantage over the Americans in the use of recorders. It was not because the technology was not available, although the German machines tended to be the best. Saerchinger had noted during his tenure as a CBS representative that the Nazi rallies and speeches were frequently rebroadcast during the evening hours if they had taken place during the afternoon. The recordings were probably made by a steel needle cutting into a wax cylinder. The cylinder could be shaved electronically and reused up to fifty times. A more recent development was the wire recorder, which did not come into general use until the end of World War II.[11]

Why the fuss over live broadcasts? There is some evidence that union contracts were one part of the requirement. Another, supported by former CBS President Frank Stanton, is that the policy stopped reporters from faking coverage. But more likely, the central reason for the ban on use of recordings was the need for credibility of the product and its immediateness. E. P. H. James, a pioneer network engineer, recalls that the policy existed even in the early days of commercial radio. "The idea at the time was that radio had to be genuine, had to be believable, had to be different from the phonograph. It wasn't canned, you see? . . . For a long while it was considered to be a sort of hoax to play on the listener, to have anything that wasn't live. I mean—this, I admit, was an extreme view—but there it was."[12]

Sometimes the rules were bent. The Hindenberg crash is the best example. And in late 1936, Senator Arthur Vandenberg proposed debating President Roosevelt in absentia—by responding live to recorded excerpts from the President's speeches. At first, CBS rejected the proposal as being a "dramatization," but then decided it could be aired.[13]

Mutual did not have a policy forbidding the use of recordings and so it did use them, mostly in such broadcasts as end-of-the-year reviews. Some indication of the influence of the youngest network was that neither CBS nor NBC felt threatened enough by MBS to change their policies.

CBS lifted the ban at the end of 1945.[14] One reason may have been the continuing problems experienced in receiving the live feeds from Europe. Sunspots were a big problem, wiping out reception for days at a time.

It so often happened that you had atmospheric conditions at night-time when Europe was covered by darkness. And America was still day. You had trouble transmitting signals. What Ed and I tried to do was get them to record in New York. If we broadcast there at midnight European time, it would be six or seven in the evening in New York, and then if it didn't come through, try it again, but they wouldn't do that. So what often happened was that the moment we came through, at whatever time of night it was, they couldn't get our signal so they didn't have any broadcast.[15]

While NBC carried all of its correspondents' reports live in 1940, the network engineers did record many of the pieces as they came in. If the recording engineer thought the piece was especially good, he might play it back for MacVane on the cue channel. Most of the recordings were on glass records and few of them have survived. CBS apparently did not do this, for Murrow did not hear his famous rooftop broadcasts until a quarter century after they were done.[16]

The broadcasts were all done at the various government facilities. And those agencies set up any remote equipment needed by the network men and women. Before the Blitz brought extensive bombing to London, CBS and NBC did a half-hour report which White judged as one of the three best European broadcasts since the start of the fighting almost a year before.[17]

Part of the "London after Dark" series, it featured nine microphones at various spots in London, with the announcer beginning by saying only "This is London calling." Soon street sounds were heard, and then Murrow—from a rooftop—described an unexpected bombing attack, his delivery crisp, demeanor authoritative. Larry Lesueur reported from an Air Raid Precaution Force headquarters, his script well written, the delivery pale in comparison to Murrow's. Sevareid was next from Hammersmith Dance Hall, sounding very young. Fred Bate reported from Buckingham Palace, his delivery theatrical and dull. Some Canadian broadcasters and a couple of British ones rounded out the program on that August 24.

The rooftop from which Murrow spoke was not at the main BBC building but, rather, a few blocks away. Prior to receiving approval for the rooftop reports, the network correspondents had done their broadcasts from the safety of a studio, while the BBC technicians turned up the volume on a microphone they had put on the roof of Broadcasting House.

The studio itself was in the basement and often was fragrant with the smells of a nearby cafeteria, particularly when the cooks were boiling cabbage. The aroma was also compounded at times by a dispensary which was down the hall. At one point during the Blitz, when people could not get back to their homes after work, Murrow broadcast with nine people lying in the studio, most of them asleep. Prior to conversion to Studio B–4, the space had been a "waitresses' robing room," which Murrow clarified as being "a lady's lavatory."[18]

While MacVane and Murrow lived within a few blocks of the BBC, Bate and Sevareid and Lesueur all lived across the street.

Each had some close calls. Lesueur had originally rented a flat which was the top floor of a building in Portland Place. When shrapnel from ack-acks fell, they burned through his roof. So he requested a lower location in the building, and was given a flat which had previously been the quarters of Somerset Maugham. It was quite opulent but was destroyed in an attack which also did great damage to the BBC. Lesueur was in the basement studios at the time and was not hurt. "Another attack nearly wiped out the entire crew for CBS. Ed, Larry Lesueur, and I filed out of the BBC and around to the side. We heard nothing, but Murrow suddenly stepped into a doorway, and Larry and I immediately followed suit. At that moment, a jagged casing from an antiaircraft shell crashed precisely where we had been."[19]

Murrow was not the only one allowed to do the rooftop broadcasts. Bate and MacVane were also allowed to do them. MacVane believes it was because of their relationship with the censors. "Censorship authorities in those days knew that we knew just about as much as they did about censorship. We were not going to say "Such and such a bomb has just landed in the middle of Picadilly Circus" or anything like that, to give away how accurate those people were in their bombing. It was a question of trusting us because we'd had so much experience that they would allow us to go on without censorship to describe things like that."[20]

Murrow was not entirely taken with the British censorship, although he realized it was mild compared to what his colleagues in Europe had been facing. "After more than a year of practice, the system remains unpredictable and erratic. It is still the most liberal system of censorship in Europe, but sometimes, in an effort to mislead Britain's enemies, it succeeds only in misleading or confusing her friends."[21]

A more restrictive policy would have hurt, rather than helped, the British cause. There were 120 American foreign correspondents covering the Blitz from the British side of the channel.

In one of Murrow's first broadcasts from the top of the BBC building in Portland Place, he demonstrated the trust was well placed and that the practice had paid off. "I'm standing on a rooftop looking out over London. At the moment everything is quiet. For reasons of national as well as personal security, I'm unable to tell you the exact location from where I'm speaking. Off to my left, far away in the distance, I can see just that faint red angry snap of antiaircraft bursts against the steel-blue sky, but the guns are so far away that it's impossible to hear them from this location."[22] Murrow continued his description while German planes passed overhead and the British antiaircraft gunners tried to shoot them down.

Murrow had long before come to some personal conclusions about the Germans and the British, and they were intensified as the bombs fell on England. In a letter to his wife, who was taking a rest in the country from the worst of the London bombing, he wrote about his performance: "Have been doing some fair talking last few nights. Pulled out all the stops and let them have it. Now I think is the time. A thousand years of history and civilization are being smashed."[23]

On the air, he continued to practice journalistic habits which set him apart from most of the other foreign correspondents. In particular, many of his reports talked about how the common man was taking it.

The reporter must never sound excited, even if bombs are falling outside. Rather, the reporter should imagine that he has just returned to his hometown and that the local editor has asked him to dinner with a banker and a professor. After dinner your host asks you, "Well, what was it like?" As you talk, the maid is passing the coffee and her boyfriend, a truck driver, is waiting for her in the kitchen and listening. You are supposed to describe things in terms that make sense to the truck driver without insulting the intelligence of the professor.[24]

In early September, the German focus turned from the coastal areas of England to London. On Black Saturday, September 7, 1940, between 5 and 6 P.M., 320 German bombers supported by 600 fighter planes followed the Thames toward London. They bombed Woolwich Arsenal, the Beckton Gas Works, the East Surrey Commercial Docks, and then the West Ham power station, the old City of London, Westminster, and finally Kensington. At 8:10 P.M., 250 more bombers appeared over the area, and the attacks continued until 4:30 A.M. The death toll was 430, with 1,600 seriously wounded.

MacVane and his wife had been out on that beautiful Saturday afternoon, looking at some damage done in a preliminary
bombing a day or two before near the Elephant and Castle underground station. When the air raid sirens first sounded, the
MacVanes took refuge in a doorway with a policeman. When
the bombs started falling, they went into the house itself, the
occupants having left it unlocked. Lucy was sent back to the
BBC to fill in NBC and BBC reporters on what they had witnessed, while John made his way closer to a huge fire in the
docks area. He met a young reporter, Vivien Batcheler, of the
Daily Sketch, and together they ducked the bombs and watched
the inferno. Then they started to leave to make their deadlines.

We started to walk, the bombs coming fast now. About every 100 or
200 yards, we would hear the express train rush of the bomb. We would
duck into a doorway. Vivien would lie down, and I would flop on top
of her, instinctively. As the sound of falling debris came to our ears,
we would pick ourselves up and start moving on. No traffic was in
the streets. We were all alone. . . . We had to walk all the way to
London Bridge, a matter of at least three miles, before we saw any
cars moving. There, by some luck, we got a taxi. I put my arm around
Vivien and held her close all the way back to the office. For the moment I felt closer to her than to any other woman in the world except
Lucy, yet we knew nothing about each other except that we had shared
one terrible night of fear together. . . . I got back to the BBC exhausted. In the studio were Fred Bate and James Reston of the *New
York Times*, who shared Fred's apartment. . . . It was ten minutes to
one, and we were due on the air at one-fifteen. I slumped in a chair
and told Fred Bate that I was so tired I could not go on.[25]

Bate assured MacVane that just three minutes of eyewitness
description would do—he and Reston would handle the details
of the attack. Because a censorship ban on news of the dock
fires had just been lifted, MacVane's report was the first account of the inferno sent to America.

Murrow had also watched the dock fire, but from a distance.
He and print correspondents Vincent Sheean and Ben Robert-
son had gone to Gravesend and watched the first wave of
bombers as they came in. Later, they saw the pilots of succes-
sive waves of bombers using the fires as guidepoints for their
nighttime runs. The trio remained in a ditch near an airfield for

most of the night, taking a room at an inn as the bombing decreased, and returning to London the next morning.

That night, Murrow and MacVane were having a drink at a pub near their homes. Murrow invited the MacVanes to spend the evening at his flat. Later, as the Murrows and MacVanes were working their way through a bottle of scotch, the bombing came nearer—and then a big one hit just a few blocks away. The two reporters ran to Murrow's car and drove over to have a look at the fires caused by the explosion. They did not have broadcasts scheduled—it was Sunday night in London—and so they went back to the flat. The raid continued until morning again, and the death toll this time was 412.

For the rest of September, the German bombers flew over London daily. During those twenty-three days the correspondents in London told America about what it was like to be bombed without surcease. Murrow seemed to enjoy challenging death; he took risks and went where he did not have to go. Sevareid did not enjoy it. "The time came when I found myself unable to tolerate the shaking room, and when there was no broadcast errand to run I found myself going down to the basement shelter, which seemed somehow ignoble. There were days when even in the quiet I could not align my thoughts nor summon energy for the most trivial tasks. At times I felt myself the victim of an incomprehensible trance, and the high historic meaning of fierce events could not break through the corroded consciousness."[26]

The bombings also had a very sobering effect on MacVane. "I do not think any of us really expected to live through the war. Life seemed very tenuous indeed. The worst feature was the constant strain. Unless you have experienced something like that, a prolonged period in which all your ordinary assurance of living has disappeared and you must face the fact that at any hour of the day or night death may come to you in an instant, I do not think you have obtained full self-knowledge. Most men live their lives without knowing how they would act in an ultimate crisis."[27]

Murrow would later say that he had left his youth and part of his heart in England when he returned to America after the war to become a CBS executive. Little known is that he had an opportunity to stay in Britain as one of the top men in the BBC. Murrow considered it seriously enough to go back to the United States in the summer of 1943 and talk the offer over with several friends, including Supreme Court Justice Felix Frankfurter.[28]

MacVane, too, came to love the British people for their courage: "London's ordeal was an easy story to write—one could almost have written it by sitting in a basement night and day and reading the papers—but we broadcasters had so identified ourselves with the people of London that we did not feel we could shirk any of their experiences. We rode the ambulances, visited gun sites, and watched firemen at work. Our country was neutral, but we ourselves, for that reason, had to prove to our British colleagues and the people with whom we lived that we were willing to share their lives completely."[29]

The networks' coverage was receiving attention, and even awards. In October, Murrow was named a winner of the Overseas Press Club of America award. Listed as close runners-up, along with some print journalists, were the NBC European staff and William L. Shirer. The CBS man in Berlin did win an award also, in 1940. It was the Headliner's Club Award.[30]

As fall turned to winter, the Nazi bombing began to decrease. The London fog came to the air of the city whose population was less than half what it had been a year earlier. Those who were there had made a stand which was unlike any previous one. They could not see the enemy face to face, but they fought well enough to begin to turn the tide against the Nazis.

Sevareid, who was sick and tired—sick from an illness he had apparently been fighting since Paris fell, and tired of the bombing—wanted to return to the United States. "I was both ill and homesick and of no great use in the postcrisis days of pure endurance which were coming. I had been away for three years and knew little of what my people were thinking, of whether I was doing this unfamiliar work properly or not."[31]

Sevareid sent a final broadcast to America, one which caused many of those who heard it to understand better the man who made it and the story he had reported. Sevareid was the first to go home. But he was followed by Shirer, Bate, and Jordan by the end of winter. Shirer had continued to have trouble with the Nazi censors through the summer of 1940. On September 2, he wrote that he had been forbidden to use the word "Nazi" in his broadcasts because it had a bad sound in America. Two weeks later, he was informed that newspaper headlines from German papers could not be included in his reports. They, too, gave American listeners "a wrong impression," said the censors. He felt the situation was becoming impossible.

On October 15, 1940, Shirer decided to send his family from Switzerland to America. The Germans were cutting down on shipments of food and coal to the Swiss, and life even in that neutral country would be difficult for his wife and little daughter in the coming winter. Also, Shirer felt the routes for possible escape from Switzerland were going to be increasingly limited as the Nazi territory expanded. And he made plans to go, too: "I shall follow in December. I think my usefulness here is just about over. Until recently, despite the censorship, I think I've been able to do an honest job of reporting from Germany. But it has become increasingly difficult and at present it has become almost impossible."[32] Shirer had come to feel that life had little value in Germany by then, and he felt there was no more job for him under those circumstances. Jordan had come to a similar conclusion. While the German invasion of the Low Countries was underway, the Nazis instituted a procedure which required four copies of every proposed script and the okay of three different agencies—propaganda, foreign, and military. The veteran NBC man felt he was involved from then on in "shadowboxing," with the Nazis watching him for just one false step.

Jordan had gotten on the Nazi "blacklist" for a number of reasons. In addition to associating with democrats at the Friday luncheon club, he had also made a habit of comparing pre-Nazi Germany to the current conditions under Hitler. He attempted to help Jews leave Germany prior to the declaration of war, and had smuggled in restricted goods for friends. When Paris fell in June, the Nazis came into possession of some information Jordan had collected about religious persecution under Hitler. He had left it with a friend, and apparently the data was to be sent on to members of the Catholic press in America. But the friend left it behind in the rush to leave Paris, and now Jordan found himself under special scrutiny. Jordan felt he was just doing his job. "It really mattered little what Himmler's sleuths thought of me. I was going about the legitimate business of a radio reporter. Information I could obtain from confidential sources was a prerequisite of my job. Had our broadcasts merely consisted of what propaganda was handed over, they would have been meager enough."[33]

Jordan, with help from Archinard, who was by then in Vichy France for NBC, broadcast the dismissal of Pierre Laval in December 1940. He did his report from Basel, and commented freely on the implications of the shake-up by Pétain. The broadcast so infuriated the Nazis that a formal protest was launched in Washington, and the Germans intimated that Jordan would soon be banned from Nazi territory. For certain, he would be denied interviews with government and military officials, would not be able to go to the front, and would have difficulty in getting anything more than the most nominal cooperation from RRG authorities. Jordan closed the office in Basel, and shortly after the end of the year, he returned to America. Jordan was replaced by Charles Lanius in January 1941.

Shirer was already gone by then. Murrow had gone to see him off on December 8. The two men talked of what they had accomplished since 1937, staying up until 5 A.M. one day, and taking a brief five-day vacation together. They went to the Portuguese beach, but mostly drank and talked. On December 13, Shirer's ship sailed from Lisbon. It was an emotional parting. "All day both of us depressed at leaving, for we have worked together very closely, Ed and I, during the last three turbulent years over here, and a bond grew that was very real, a kind you only make a few times in your life, and somehow, absurdly no doubt, sentimentally perhaps, we had a presentiment that the fortunes of war, maybe just a little bomb, would make this reunion the last."[34]

It was not the last, although there would be more close calls for Murrow. After the war, there would be great bitterness between the two men. Murrow, a chief of CBS news, would be involved in a controversy over Shirer's commentary which ended in Shirer's resignation. In 1954, *Stranger Come Home* by Shirer was seen as a thinly veiled attack on Murrow's actions while a CBS vice-president.

Perhaps their presentiment had been colored by a telegram Murrow received while in Portugal. On the night of December 8, the area around the BBC had been rocked by a magnetic mine which exploded in Langham Place. At least one policeman was killed, and Fred Bate was seriously injured along with twenty-four others.

Bate had been preparing a broadcast at his desk in the NBC office at 11 Portland Place, which also doubled as his home, when the blast occurred about 11 P.M. He recalled the impact as feeling "like all of London was pouring in the window."[35] Bate had serious head and leg wounds and was wandering around the office in shock when two NBC secretaries, who had been in the safety of the BBC basement when the mine went off, found him.

The CBS offices, also on Portland Place, were demolished. Lesueur planned to go ahead with his broadcast from the BBC basement, but water began to seep through from above. He got his British censor to get in a cab with him and head down for Bush House, where master control was. "We got down to around Picadilly, and the censor said he had to get out, he was too shaken by the bombing. The cabdriver was one of those plucky British cabdrivers, and he took me down to Bush House. I went upstairs to broadcast, but the duty officer said I couldn't do it without the censor. So all I could do was when the time came for the broadcast tell CBS in New York, Paul White, that I could not go on."[36]

The bombing in December was not the first time the network offices had been damaged. Sevareid recalls an earlier office in Langham Place being hit in the summer while he and Murrow were sitting in the Langham Hotel, across the street from the BBC. The CBS Duchess Street office was also damaged during the Blitz, and both networks had their offices damaged at least once before the bombing ended. Murrow is reported to have lost a journal in one of the later demolishings, which may be one reason why he did not write something similar to books done by other correspondents.[37]

NBC got a new office at 1 Duchess Street, and MacVane took over the bureau from Bate. After several weeks in the hospital, Bate was released, and his doctors convinced him to return to the United States for a period of convalescence. His journey home was not a quick one. The *Yankee Clipper* flying boat was delayed in the Azores for two weeks by high waves, which prevented it from taking off, and Bate did not reach New York until the end of January. Even then he was eager to go back to England. "I am going back as soon as my holiday is over, and I am anxious to be off. Did you ever hear Beatrice Lillie sing 'Only Mad Dogs and Englishmen Sit in the Noonday Sun?' Well, they can take the sun and they can take plenty more. And I want to be there and watch them."[38] Bate did return to London in May of 1941. He left again in the summer of 1942 to be in charge of NBC's shortwave broadcasts from America.

By the end of 1940, only the *Christian Science Monitor* Berlin correspondents were allowed to broadcast for CBS. All other reporters were ordered by their wire agency and newspaper editors to stay off the air. Some felt what the editors "didn't know wouldn't hurt them." Percy Knauth of the *New York Times* broadcast from Berlin in early 1940 under the name John Anderson. And James B. Reston, also of the *Times*, reported for NBC from London, also using an assumed name.[39] After a series of reports in late 1940, "Anderson" was ordered to halt the broadcasts.

Through the winter months of 1940, and on into 1941, the bombing of London and other parts of Britain continued. So, of course, did the broadcasting back to America. The staffs overseas grew, although sometimes not as quickly as the bureau chiefs wanted.[40]

Sevareid was replaced by twenty-three-year-old Charles Collingwood, Shirer by Harry Flannery. Soon Howard K. Smith and Richard C. Hottelet would join CBS. Collectively, the CBS correspondents would come to be known as "Murrow's Boys." But the men and women who transformed foreign correspondence on the American networks were the ones who had been on the air in the summer of 1940 and before.

When they returned home, Sevareid, Shirer, Jordan, and Bate began to realize the impact their reporting had on America. Bate was interviewed after his plane landed in New York and was quoted as an authority on developments in Europe.[41]

Sevareid went to 485 Madison Avenue and met for the first

time with people to whom he had been talking daily for the past year.

The bustling, efficient offices of the broadcasting company were a little overwhelming at first, and I felt conscience stricken in the realization that so many men, so much complicated machinery, had been devoted so often to processing the brief, hesitant little speeches I had been giving from the areas of the war. To stand on a street corner and hear Larry's words, spoken at that moment in the curtained underground London studio, blaring now from the passing cars, to walk into a hotel lobby and hear Ed drawing his breath three thousand miles away—these were experiences thrilling beyond compare. I wanted to write them that the whole thing was real after all, and not pantomime in an empty room.[42]

NOTES

1. Sevareid, *Not So Wild a Dream*, p. 163.
2. John MacVane, interview with the author, January 8, 1981.
3. Ibid.
4. J. B. Priestley, *All England Listened: A Collection of J. B. Priestley's Radio Broadcast Scripts* (New York: Chilmark Press, 1967).
5. MacVane, interview with the author, January 8, 1981.
6. Sevareid, interview with the author, November 6, 1980.
7. CBS Radio Network, "Farewell to Studio Nine."
8. Kendrick, *Prime Time*, p. 207.
9. Shirer, interview with the author, October 11, 1980.
10. Shirer, *Berlin Diary*, p. 204.
11. Tony Treble, BBC Archives Librarian, interview with the author, March 1977.
12. E. P. H. James, Columbia University Oral History Collection, pp. 9 & 11.
13. Barnouw, *The Golden Web*, p. 52.
14. *Broadcasting*, November 17, 1945.
15. Shirer, interview with the author, October 11, 1980.
16. CBS Radio Network, "Farewell to Studio Nine."
17. The other two were Shirer and Keirker from Compiègne and William L. White's Christmas broadcast.
18. CBS Radio Network, "Farewell to Studio Nine."
19. Sevareid, *Not So Wild a Dream*, p. 170.
20. MacVane, interview with the author, January 8, 1981.

21. Hall, *This Is London*, p. 211.
22. Ibid., p. 195.
23. Kendrick, *Prime Time*, p. 208.
24. Gordon and Falk, *On the Spot Reporting*, p. 30.
25. John MacVane, *On the Air in World War II* (New York: Morrow, 1979), p. 23.
26. Sevareid, *Not So Wild a Dream*, p. 170.
27. MacVane, *On the Air in World War II*, p. 32.
28. Joseph P. Lash, *From the Diaries of Felix Frankfurter* (New York: Norton, 1975), pp. 256–57.
29. MacVane, *On the Air in World War II*, p. 36.
30. *New York Times*, October 2, 1940, p. 21; and Christopher Tunney, *A Biographical Dictionary of World War II* (New York: St. Martin's Press, 1972), p. 172.
31. Sevareid, *Not So Wild a Dream*, p. 179.
32. Shirer, *Berlin Diary*, p. 543.
33. Jordan, *Beyond All Fronts*, p. 293.
34. Shirer, *Berlin Diary*, pp. 602–4.
35. *New York Times*, February 1, 1941, p. 2.
36. Larry Lesueur, interview with the author, November 26, 1982.
37. Kendrick, *Prime Time*, p. 210.
38. Lanfranco Rasponi, "Reporting Under Fire," *New York Times*, sect. 10, p. 10, February 16, 1941.
39. Flannery, *Assignment to Berlin*, p. 35.
40. MacVane, *On the Air in World War II*, p. 112.
41. "Britain Held Eager for Nazi Invasion," *New York Times*, February 1, 1941, p. 2.
42. Sevareid, *Not So Wild a Dream*, p. 184.

· Bibliography

BOOKS

Allen, Fred. *Treadmill to Oblivion*. Boston: Little, Brown, 1954.

Allen, Frederick Lewis. *Since Yesterday: The Nineteen-Thirties in America*. 1940. Reprint. New York: Bantam, 1965.

Altheide, David L. *Creating Reality: How TV Distorts Events*. Beverly Hills, Calif.: Sage, 1974.

Baden, Anne L. *Radio and Television Broadcasting in the United States and Foreign Countries*. Washington, D.C.: Library of Congress, 1941.

Barnouw, Erik. *A Tower in Babel: A History of Broadcasting in the United States to 1933*. New York: Oxford University Press, 1966.

————. *The Golden Web: A History of Broadcasting in the United States, 1933–1953*. New York: Oxford University Press, 1968.

Bartlett, Vernon. *Intermission in Europe: The Life of a Journalist and Broadcaster*. New York: Oxford University Press, 1938.

Bendiner, Robert. *Just around the Corner—a Highly Selective History of the 30's*. New York: Harper & Row, 1967.

Benjamin, Robert Spiers. *The Inside Story*. New York: Prentice-Hall, 1940.

Bliss, Edward W., Jr. *In Search of Light: The Broadcasts of Edward R. Murrow, 1938–1961*. New York: Knopf, 1967.

Briggs, Asa. *The Golden Age of Wireless*. London: Oxford University Press, 1965.

British Broadcasting Corporation. *British Broadcasting: A Bibliography*. London: BBC, 1954.

Brooks, John. *The Great Leap: The Past 25 Years in America*. New York: Harper & Row, 1966.

Brown, Cecil B. *Suez to Singapore*. New York: Random House, 1942.

Burlingame, Roger. *Don't Let Them Scare You: The Life and Times of Elmer Davis*. Philadelphia: Lippincott, 1961.

Cantril, Hadley. *The Invasion from Mars: A Study in the Psychology of Panic*. Princeton: Princeton University Press, 1940.

154   Bibliography

Charnley, Mitchell V. *News by Radio*. New York: Macmillan, 1948.
———. *Reporting*. New York: Holt-Dryden, 1959.
Churchill, Winston. *The Gathering Storm*. Boston: Houghton Mifflin, 1948.
Cohen, Bernard C. *The Press and Foreign Police*. Princeton: Princeton University Press, 1963.
Cohen, Stanley, and Jack Young, eds. *The Manufacture of News*. Beverly Hills, Calif.: Sage, 1973.
Cole, J. A. *Lord Haw-Haw and William Joyce*. New York: Farrar, Strauss & Giroux, 1964.
Columbia Broadcasting System. *Vienna*. Edited by Paul Keston and Victor Ratner. New York: CBS, March 1938.
———. *Crisis*. Edited by Victor Ratner and Jules Dundes. New York: CBS, December 1938.
Culbert, David Holbrook. *News for Everyman: Radio and Foreign Affairs in Thirties America*. Westport, Conn.: Greenwood Press, 1976.
Daniels, Jonathan. *The Time between the Wars: From the Jazz Age and the Depression to Pearl Harbor*. Garden City, N.Y.: Doubleday, 1966.
Dary, David. *Radio News Handbook*. Thurmont, Md.: TAB Books, 1967.
Desmond, Robert W. *The Information Progress: World News Reporting to the Twentieth Century*. Iowa City, Iowa: University of Iowa Press, 1978.
Dimbleby, Jonathan. *Richard Dimbleby*. London: Coronet, 1975.
Dryer, Sherman H. *Radio in Wartime*. New York: Greenberg, 1942.
Dunlap, Orrin C., Jr. *Radio and Television Almanac*. New York: Harper, 1951.
Etheridge, James M., ed. *Current Biography*. Detroit: Gale Research Co., 1962.
Fielding, Raymond. *The American Newsreel, 1911–1967*. Norman, Okla.: University of Oklahoma Press, 1964.
Flannery, Harry W. *Assignment to Berlin*. New York: Knopf, 1942.
Gans, Herbert J. *Deciding What's News: A Study of CBS Evening News, NBC Nightly News, Newsweek and Time*. New York: Pantheon, 1979.
Gates, Gary P. *Air Time: The Inside Story of CBS News*. New York: Harper & Row, 1978.
Gordon, George N., and Irving A. Falk. *On the Spot Reporting: Radio Records History*. New York: J. Messner, 1967.
Graves, Harold N., Jr. *War on the Short Wave*. New York: Foreign Policy Association, 1941.
Hall, F. D. M., ed. *This Is London*. New York: Simon & Schuster, 1941.
Hansen, Donald A., and Herschel J. Parsons. *Mass Communications: A Research Bibliography*. Santa Barbara, Calif.: Glendessary Press, 1968.

Hardt, Hanno. *Social Theories of the Press*. Beverly Hills, Calif.: Sage, 1979.

Head, Sydney W. *Broadcasting in America*. 2nd ed. Boston: Houghton Mifflin, 1972.

Hiett, Helen. *No Matter Where*. New York: Dutton, 1944.

Hohenberg, John. *Foreign Correspondence: The Great Reporters and Their Times*. New York: Columbia University Press, 1967.

Ireland, Norma O. *Index to Women of the World: From Ancient to Modern Times—Biographies and Portraits*. Westwood, Mass.: Faxon, 1970.

Jordan, Max. *Beyond All Fronts: A Bystander's Notes on This Thirty Years War*. Milwaukee: Bruce, 1944.

Kaltenborn, H. V. *Fifty Fabulous Years, 1900–1950: A Personal Review*. New York: Putnam, 1950.

Kendrick, Alexander. *Prime Time: The Life of Edward R. Murrow*. Boston: Little, Brown, 1969.

Koch, Howard. *The Panic Broadcast: Portrait of an Event*. Boston: Little, Brown, 1970.

Korbe, Sidney. *Foundations of American Journalism*. 1950. Reprint. Westport, Conn.: Greenwood Press, 1970.

Kunitz, Stanley J., and Howard Haycroft. *Twentieth-Century Authors*. New York: Wilson, 1942.

Lash, Joseph P. *From the Diaries of Felix Frankfurter*. New York: Norton, 1975.

MacDonald, J. Fred. *Don't Touch That Dial: Radio Programming in American Life, 1920–1960*. Chicago: Nelson-Hall, 1979.

MacVane, John. *On the Air in World War II*. New York: Morrow, 1979.

Marzolf, Marion Tuttle. *Up from the Footnote: A History of Women Journalists*. New York: Hastings House, 1977.

Mathews, Joseph J. *Reporting the Wars*. Westport, Conn.: Greenwood Press, 1957.

Metz, Robert. *CBS: Reflections in a Bloodshot Eye*. Chicago: Playboy Press, 1975.

Miller, Webb. *I Found No Peace*. New York: Simon & Schuster, 1936.

Mydans, Carl. *More Than Meets the Eye*. New York: Harper & Bros., 1959.

National Broadcasting Company. *Thirty-five Hours a Day*. New York: NBC, 1937.

Newhall, Beaumont. *The History of Photography: From 1839 to the Present Day*. New York: Museum of Modern Art, 1964.

Nippon Hoso Kyokai. *Fifty Years of Japanese Broadcasting*. Edited by the History Compilation Room, Radio and TV Culture Institute. Tokyo: NHK, 1977.

Paley, William S. *As It Happened: A Memoir.* Garden City, N.Y.: Doubleday, 1979.

Paulu, Barton. *British Broadcasting.* Minneapolis: University of Minnesota Press, 1956.

Powdermaker, Hortense. *Hollywood: The Dream Factory—an Anthropologist Looks at the Movie-Makers.* Boston: Little, Brown, 1951.

Priestley, J. B. *All England Listened: A Collection of J. B. Priestley's Radio Broadcast Scripts.* New York: Chilmark Press, 1967.

Robinson, Thomas Portes. *Radio Networks and the Federal Government.* New York: Columbia University Press, 1943.

Rogers, Everett M., with F. Floyd Shoemaker. *Communication of Innovations: A Cross-Cultural Approach.* New York: Free Press, 1971.

Rolo, Charles J. *Radio Goes to War.* New York: Putnam, 1940.

Rose, Oscar. *Radio Broadcasting and TV.* New York: Wilson, 1947.

Roshco, Bernard. *Newsmaking.* Chicago: University of Chicago Press, 1975.

Saerchinger, Cesar. *Hello America: Radio Adventures in Europe.* Boston: Houghton Mifflin, 1938.

Schechter, A. A. *Go Ahead Garrison!: A Story of News Broadcasting.* New York: Dodd, Mead, 1940.

———, with Edward Anthony. *I Live on Air.* New York: Stokes, 1941.

Schudson, Michael. *Discovering the News: A Social History of American Newspapers.* New York: Basic Books, 1978.

Sevareid, Eric. *Canoeing with the Cree.* 1935. Reprint. St. Paul: St. Paul Historical Society, 1960.

———. *Not So Wild a Dream.* New York: Knopf, 1941.

Shibutani, Tamotsu. *Improvised News: A Sociological Study of Rumor.* Indianapolis, Ind.: Bobbs-Merrill, 1966.

Shirer, William L. *Berlin Diary.* New York: Knopf, 1941.

———. *Twentieth Century Journey: A Memoir of a Life and the Times.* New York: Simon & Schuster, 1976.

Shuneman, P. Smith. *Photographic Communication.* New York: Hastings House, 1972.

Sigal, Leon V. *Reporters and Officials.* Lexington, Mass.: Heath, 1973.

Slate, Sam J., and Joe Cook. *It Sounds Impossible.* New York: Macmillan, 1963.

Smith, R. Franklin. *Edward R. Murrow: The War Years.* Kalamazoo, Mich.: New Issues Press, 1978.

Smithsonian Institution. *The Smithsonian Book of Invention.* Edited by Alexis Doster, Joe Goodwin, and Jane M. Ross. New York: Norton, 1978.

Snyder, Louis L. *The War: A Concise History, 1939–1945.* New York: J. Messner, 1960.

Bibliography   157

Stein, M. L. *Under Fire: The Story of American War Correspondents.* New York: J. Messner, 1968.

Storey, Graham. *Reuters: The Story of a Century of News Gathering.* New York: Greenwood, 1969.

Stott, William. *Documentary Expression and Thirties America.* New York: Oxford University Press, 1973.

Swing, Raymond Gram. *How War Came.* New York: Norton, 1939.

Tuchman, Gaye. *Making News.* New York: Free Press, 1978.

Tunney, Christopher. *A Biographical Dictionary of World War II.* New York: St. Martin's Press, 1972.

Tunstall, Jeremy. *Journalists at Work.* Beverly Hills, Calif.: Sage, 1971.

Waugh, Evelyn. *Scoop.* Boston: Little, Brown, 1938.

White, Paul W. *Covering a War for Radio.* New York: CBS, 1940.

———. *News on the Air.* New York: Harcourt Brace, 1947.

Wile, Frederick William. *News Is Where You Find It.* New York: Bobbs-Merrill, 1939.

Wood, William A. *Electronic Journalism.* New York: Columbia University Press, 1967.

ARTICLES

"Anatomy of a Panic," *Time,* Vol. 35, No. 16, April 15, 1940, pp. 58–61.

"And All Because They're Smart," *Fortune,* Vol. 11, June 1935, pp. 154–160.

Anderson, Russell F. "News from Nowhere," *Saturday Review of Literature,* Vol. 24, No. 46, November 17, 1951.

Breed, Warren. "Social Control in the News Room: A Functional Analysis," *Social Forces,* Vol. 33, No. 4, May 1955, p. 326.

"Britain Held Eager for Nazi Invasion," *New York Times,* February 2, 1941, p. 2.

"CBS Goes South," *Time,* Vol. 37, No. 1, January 6, 1941, p. 37.

Cleveland Plain Dealer, December 8, 1938. Untitled article.

———. June 11, 1944. Untitled article.

Davis, Elmer. "Broadcasting the Outbreak of War," *Harper's,* Vol. 179, November 1939, p. 579.

Douglas, Paul. "Short Wave Listening," *Public Opinion Quarterly,* Vol. 5, 1941.

"Edward Angley, 53, Newsman, Is Dead," *New York Times,* December 8, 1951, Sec. L, p. 11.

"Edward Klauber, C.B.S. Official, Dies," *New York Times,* September 24, 1954, p. 23.

"Edward R. Murrow, Broadcaster and Ex-Chief of the U.S.I.A., Dies,"
    New York Times, April 28, 1965, p. 1.
"Europe on the Air," *Time*, Vol. 35, No. 19, May 6, 1940, p. 42.
"Fine, Careless Rapture," *The New Yorker*, Vol. 15, No. 49, January 20,
    1940, p. 17.
"First Lady's Week," *Time*, Vol. 35, No. 16, April 15, 1940, p. 17.
Galtung, Johan, and Mari Ruge. "Structuring and Selecting News." In
    The Manufacture of News, edited by Stanley Cohen and Jack
    Young. Beverly Hills, Calif.: Sage, 1973, pp. 63–77.
Gans, Herbert J. "The Famine in American Mass-Communications Re-
    search: Comments on Hirsch, Tuchman, and Gecas," *American
    Journal of Sociology*, Vol. 77, No. 4, January 1972, p. 697.
Gray, L. C. "America's Ears," *Current History and Forum*, Vol. 52, No.
    7, January 10, 1941, p. 12.
"Hi-Yo, Chandler!," *Time*, Vol. 37, No. 23, June 9, 1941, pp. 47–48.
Kahn, E. J., Jr. "A Reporter at Large," *The New Yorker*, Vol. 16, No.
    11, April 27, 1940, pp. 39–48.
Kaltenborn, H. V. "Covering the Crisis," *Current History*, Vol. 51, No.
    2, October 1939, pp. 35–38.
Morris, Frank D. "Reporting Standards," *Reader's Digest*, Vol. 35, No.
    203, July 1939, p. 55.
"Mr. Wisecrack," *Time*, Vol. 35, No. 21, May 20, 1940, p. 51.
Muller, Edwin. "Radio and Reading," *The New Republic*, Vol. 102, No.
    8, February 19, 1940, pp. 236–37.
NBC Presents, Vol. III, No. 7, March 1941, p. 4. Untitled article.
"New Ties Are Seen in Aid to England," *New York Times*, October 18,
    1941, p. 12.
"Paul White Dies: Radio Newsman," *New York Times*, July 10, 1955, p.
    72.
Powell, Hickman. "Reporting the Crisis," *Reader's Digest*, Vol. 34, No.
    202, February 1939.
"Radio News," *New York Times*, October 2, 1940, p. 21.
"Radio Schedule," *New York Times*, May 21, 1939, Sec. 10, p. 10.
Rasponi, Lanfranco. "Reporting under Fire," *New York Times*, Febru-
    ary 16, 1941, Sec. 10, p. 10.
"Reading vs. Hearing the News," *New York Times*, February 16, 1941,
    Sec. 10, p. 10.
Schechter, Abel A. Untitled article, *Current History*, Vol. 11, No. 2, Oc-
    tober 1939, p. 36.
Shirer, William L. "Berlin Speaking," *Atlantic Monthly*, Vol. 168, No.
    3, September 1941, pp. 303–17.
Wertenbaker, Charles. "The World on His Back," *The New Yorker*, Vol.
    29, No. 45, December 26, 1953.

White, E. B. "Elmer Davis," *The New Yorker*, Vol. 30, No. 1, February 20, 1954.
"Yankee Accents in the Axis," *Newsweek*, Vol. 17, No. 11, March 17, 1941, p. 64.

INTERVIEWS AND ORAL HISTORIES

Breckinridge, Mary Marvin, Former CBS Amsterdam Correspondent. Interviewed May 10, 1981, and November 12, 1981.
Brown, Cecil, former CBS Rome Bureau chief. Interviewed January 30, 1981.
Bryson, Lyman, former CBS consultant for programming. Columbia University Oral History Collection (CUOHC), New York.
Dundes, Jules, formerly Of the CBS promotion department. Interviewed July 25, 1980, and September 24, 1980.
Hartrich, Edwin, former CBS correspondent. Interviewed July 17, 1981.
Hill, Russell, former CBS Berlin correspondent. Interviewed October 14, 1982.
Howe, Quincy, former commentator for CBS and MBS. CUOHC, New York.
James, E. P. H., former CBS engineer. CUOHC, New York.
Kaltenborn, H. V., former CBS and NBC commentator. CUOHC, New York.
Koch, Howard, author of "The War of the Worlds" script. Interviewed March 29, 1981.
Lesueur, Larry, former CBS London correspondent. Interviewed November 24, 1982, and November 26, 1982.
MacVane, John, former NBC London correspondent. Interviewed January 8, 1981.
Mozley, Don, former CBS San Francisco and Pacific Theater correspondent. Interviewed January 20, 1981.
Murrow, Janet, wife of Edward R. Murrow. Interviewed April 17, 1981.
Prince, Burroughs, former NBC foreign news editor. Interviewed January 27, 1981.
Schechter, Abel A., former NBC news director. Interviewed April 4, 1981.
Sevareid, Eric, former CBS Paris bureau chief and London correspondent. Interviewed October 1976 and November 6, 1980.
Seward, James, former CBS assistant treasurer. Interviewed January 31, 1981.
Shirer, William L., former CBS Berlin bureau Chief. Interviewed October 11, 1980.

Stanton, Frank, former CBS president. Interviewed January 8, 1981.
Thomas, Lowell, former CBS and NBC commentator. Interviewed October 30, 1980.
Treble, Tony, BBC archivist. Interviewed March 1977.
Wason, Betty, former CBS Athens correspondent. Interviewed June 5, 1981, and December 26, 1981.
Woodward, Margaret Rupli, former NBC Amsterdam correspondent. Interviewed May 21, 1981, and December 26, 1981.

BROADCASTS AND RECORDINGS

"CBS Radio at 50," Columbia Broadcasting System, September 18, 1977.
"Crisis: Voices and Sounds of Events That Created History," Decca, DXB 194.
"Edward R. Murrow, I Can Hear It Now: 1919–1949," Columbia Records, D3L 366.
"Edward R. Murrow, I Can Hear It Now: 1930–1945," Columbia Records, ML 4095.
"Farewell to Studio Nine," Columbia Broadcasting System, July 26, 1964.
"Hark! the Years," Capitol Records, Cap. T2334.
"Options: In Memory of Edward R. Murrow," Public Broadcasting System, April 20, 1980.
"Over Easy: Eric Sevareid Interviewed by Hugh Downs," Public Broadcasting System, February 28, 1980.
"Thirty-five Eventful Years," Radio Station WJR, Detroit, May 4, 1957.
"This Is Edward R. Murrow," Columbia Broadcasting System, April 30, 1965.
"The War of the Worlds," Columbia Broadcasting System, October 30, 1938.

· Index

About the Author

David H. Hosley is Assistant Professor in the College of Journalism at the University of Florida, Gainesville, and news director of WRUF AM-FM, Gainesville. Among his other broadcast experiences, he was a bureau chief for KCBS in San Francisco. He has published articles in *feed/back,* the *California Journalism Review, Historical Journal of Film, Radio and Television,* and *World Encounter.*